From

MANAGER *to*
EXECUTIVE

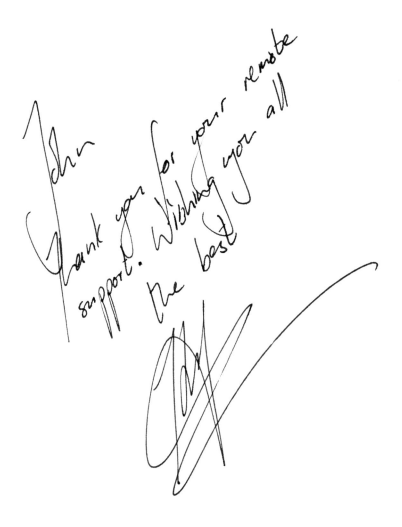

John

Thank you for your remote support. Wishing you all the best

From
MANAGER *to*
EXECUTIVE
Take your career to the next level

BY TOM GARDNER

GRAMMAR
FACTORY
— EST. 2013 —

Published by Grammar Factory Publishing, an imprint of MacMillan Company Limited.

Grammar Factory Publishing
MacMillan Company Limited
25 Telegram Mews, 39th Floor, Suite 3906
Toronto, Ontario, Canada
M5V 3Z1

www.grammarfactory.com

Gardner, Tom.
From Manager to Executive: Take Your Career to the Next Level / Tom Gardner.

Paperback ISBN 978-1-998756-91-9
eBook ISBN 978-1-998756-92-6

    1. BUS071000 BUSINESS & ECONOMICS / Leadership.
    2. BUS041000 BUSINESS & ECONOMICS / Management.
    3. BUS012000 BUSINESS & ECONOMICS / Careers / General.

Production Credits
Edited by Kate Rears
Cover design by Designerbility
Interior layout design by Ashley Howell
Book production, publication and distribution by Grammar Factory Publishing

Grammar Factory's Carbon Neutral Publishing Commitment
Grammar Factory Publishing is proud to be neutralizing the carbon footprint of all printed copies of its authors' books printed by or ordered directly through Grammar Factory or its affiliated companies through the purchase of Gold Standard-Certified International Offsets.

"In theory, there is no difference between theory and practice. But, in practice, there is."

- JAN LA VAN DE SNEPSCHEUT

PREFACE

I was sitting in a working session with the CEO of one of the world's largest beverage companies. I was 25 years old.

This wasn't a presentation. We were four hours into what would turn out to be a six-hour strategy session. This CEO, let's call her Norma, was notorious for three things: Knowing every inch of the business, not having any breaks in meetings, and smoking.

Like a hitman, Norma was brought in to clean-up-shop when the board needed tighter, more efficient operations. And, knowing every inch of the organization from decades of experience, Norma had everyone in the organization on their toes—especially the catwalk-worthy PAs hired by her predecessor.

Norma didn't stop for anything. If you needed the bathroom, you held it in until the last possible minute for fear of missing something important. If Norma needed the bathroom, she got up and walked out. This had an effect like pushing pause during a film: The room stopped mid-sentence and waited in silence for her return.

Norma always chose a particular boardroom for these sessions.

It had wide doors opening onto a large, inner atrium filled with foliage. Norma's get-shit-done silhouette spent the bulk of those meetings standing at those doors, cigarette smoke trailing off into the atrium.

Mid-interrogation, Norma asked: "How many shifts did you model for those production lines?"

"Three shifts of eight hours per day," I replied, "24/7 operations."

"Well, you should have modeled four!" was Norma's response.

From the Valley of Despair, all I can remember thinking is: "What the hell am I doing here…?!?"

What follows in this book are the learnings I've obtained from a career of working with top executives and climbing the ladder to executive myself.

I have gained numerous insights from working alongside some amazing executives, and my fair share of terrible ones. First, as a consultant with McKinsey & Company, and then as COO and Co-CEO of various businesses, and as a strategic adviser.

WHAT DO EXECUTIVES DO? AND WHAT DO EXECUTIVES THINK AND WORRY ABOUT?

These are two questions that have always interested me and others like me. Thankfully, I got my fair share of answers early in my career.

Seeking the answers to these kinds of questions has always been part of my DNA—from as early as my university years.

In the third year of my engineering degree, the mental smoke started to lift: I finally had a clearer view of how the engineering program was structured; how the different years came together at a macro level; how the different engineering paths were designed to converge and diverge over time. I remember thinking: "Why didn't anyone explain this to us three years ago?"

So, I launched a mentorship program with the Engineering Faculty. I recruited third- and fourth-year engineering students and set up a formal program. We helped engineering students navigate their first year so they were better set up for early success. This, and many other onboarding programs I've designed, was founded on the question:

WHAT DO I WISH I HAD KNOWN ON DAY 1?

One of the key elements that made the mentorship program work was that it was run by students—students who had been through the system and could relate and empathize with the mindset of the first-year student.

I carried my line of questioning with me to McKinsey: What do consulting companies do with young professionals that so rapidly puts them in a position to sit among the world's most powerful executives and to have meaningful conversations with them?

Over and above the intense demands of being a McKinsey consultant, this led me to become involved in firm learning. I led early-tenure learning for my McKinsey office and was part of the global faculty—running cohort-based training weeks around the world. I also spent four months as an internal consultant, working on an internal productivity initiative called Engagement 3.0. The aim of this program was to distill and codify project best practices and roll them out to engagement managers across the firm.

In this book, I explore my learnings from these, and myriad other experiences.

So, fast forwarding a couple of decades, how did we get here?

Post McKinsey, I ended up in startups, which involved a great mix of strategy work, having real responsibility, and being able to see the direct impact I produced. I love building businesses and I love building management teams.

In my third startup (the second one I had co-founded), the topic of management development came up. With my consulting experience, being relatively good at managing people, and having done so much training and coaching in my career, I was always the go-to person on management development and training. This meant I designed and delivered tailored training to my management teams.

Now working in a global business across numerous time zones, this would be impractical. I reached out to my network, across corporates and startups, to find out what management training courses they send their managers on, and if they are beneficial. From San Francisco to London to Sydney, the answers were the same:

> *We send our team on management training, but the feedback is always "it's too basic," or "it's repetitive" or "it's over-simplified."*

A significant gap was emerging from this feedback, one that I was trying to fill.

The new manager cohort is well served with topics such as how to have a one-on-one, being a good listener, and the important/urgent time management matrix. New managers have a plethora of checklists at their disposal.

At the other end of the spectrum, executive development is a big money spinner. From global consulting firms to ivy-league universities—pricey personal transformation journeys for executives abound.

So, where is the gap? Intermediate management development is the gap.

INTERMEDIATE MANAGERS ARE THE CRITICAL KINK IN THE HOURGLASS BETWEEN EXECUTIVE STRATEGY AND OPERATIONAL GETTING-STUFF-DONE.

Intermediate managers know how to have a one-on-one. They've seen the feedback model. Listening skills? Done. They've also seen some stuff. They've worked for a variety of bosses and are developing their own authentic management and leadership style. But what's next for them? What is their path to the C-Suite? Where do they find the elusive "Executive Toolkit"? How do we develop them?

These are the topics we will tackle in *From Manager to Executive*.

We can learn, from high-performing senior managers and executives, to distill what it takes to be a dynamic, senior people leader and get the right stuff done. We can also draw from the techniques and concepts that empower strategy consultants to work across all industries and functions, to serve these business leaders on strategic problems and projects. In doing so, we can begin to answer:

- What makes an executive tick?

- What is this executive focused on and what do they worry about?

- What are the broader perspectives and approaches that transcend portfolios and apply to any executive?

From Manager to Executive explores the answers to these questions to make you a better executive manager and to start closing the gap between you and the boardroom.

CONTENTS

Preface ix

INTRODUCTION 1

UNDER NEW MANAGEMENT 9

THE EXECUTIVE MINDSET 17
An Insider's Guide to the Executive Reality 18
What is the Executive Mindset? 27

THE 5S MODEL OF EXECUTIVE THINKING 31

MANAGE SELF 35
Building Trust and Emotional Bank Accounts 37
Personality and Leadership Profiles 41
Your Authentic Leadership Style And Story 50
Your Leadership Heatmap 56

MANAGE STRATEGY 63
The Strategic Process 64
Cascading Strategic Direction 72
Driving Focus with Objectives and Key Result (OKRs) 87
Executive Problem Solving 91
Reporting Strategic Progress and Managing Up 108

MANAGE STAFF 115
The Role of a Manager 116
Organizational Structure 120
Executive Heatmapping 123
Building Your Team 125
The Recruiting Process 130
Onboarding and Ramp-Up 136
Management Operating Systems 141

Trust, Candor and Crucial Conversations   148
Balcony and Dance and Backstage Management   153
Managing Individuals   157
Motivating Staff   163
Stress and Resilience   166

MANAGE SYNERGY   **175**
The T of Management   176
Collaboration and Influence   178
Designing Effective Workshops   187
Designing Effective Offsites   192

MANAGE STYLE   **201**
Inspirational Leadership and Followership   203
Engaging with Impact   211
Being Interesting   222

CONCLUSION: THE 5S ECOSYSTEM   **229**

EXECUTIVE THINKING CHECK LIST   **233**

Next Steps   **235**

About the Author   **237**

INTRODUCTION

MANAGEMENT TRAINING IS EITHER TOO BASIC, OVER-SIMPLIFIED OR REPETITIVE." This is the resounding feedback I received when I started reaching out to my network around the world, looking for good management training programs. Whether it was executives, senior managers or intermediate managers who had just come out of leadership training—the overall satisfaction levels were dismal.

This was annoying. I was then co-founder of my third startup, and, again, I would have to develop and deliver training to my team. Don't get me wrong, I love developing and delivering high-impact training. I've been doing it as a consultant, manager and executive for years. But I was disappointed that no one had developed a good intermediate manager offering that I could leverage. Whether I spoke to corporate leaders with massive budgets, dynamic startups with loads of funding, or small business leaders who were struggling with key management capabilities—no one had a good approach to core intermediate manager development.

Some of the biggest disappointments came from management training survivors themselves. I sat in a strategy workshop discussing the need to focus on important business issues and a senior manager waved a post-it note, exclaiming: *"I wasted four days in super-expensive leadership training and all I got was maybe three good takeaways. It could have been a blog post!"* It's embarrassing. On one hand you want to develop your managers and give them access to great training. On the other, *what's worse: no training or shit training...?*

We have a lot to explore. But, first, let me explain how I got to this point.

I was born to be a COO. I grew up in a lower-middle income household in South Africa—too many kids, not enough careers. There was only one way out of that small town and that was to get a scholarship.

Engineering it was. And not just any engineering, I landed a scholarship to study civil engineering. This is the kind of engineering where you hope to someday design and build skyscrapers, flyovers and the Hoover Dam. Well, in my hometown continent of Africa, many civil engineers end up working hundreds of miles from civilization, with scores of construction workers—none of whom speak English—to build a highway. On one such site, at 20 years old, I was working with a team that spoke Afrikaans and Shangaan. South Africa has 11 official languages and Shangaan is not one of them. Shangaan is a language that was developed decades ago on the mines. As workers were attracted (pronounced "enslaved") from all sorts of cultures and tribes, they developed a mixed dialect of their own. And that was Shangaan.

It was here—in temperatures over 116°F, putting down asphalt of over 200°F, speaking Afrikaans—that I had one of life's little epiphanies:

EVERY SINGLE SIGNIFICANT BUSINESS IN THE WORLD RELIES ON GETTING PEOPLE TO DO STUFF.

This planted the seed that to achieve in any field, I would have to learn how to manage people effectively. I wouldn't need to know the answers to everything. I would need to manage and orchestrate those who did.

I finished my initial engineering degree and went on to complete a master's degree. While doing my master's, I realized that I knew nothing about interest rates and economics. I knew how to think like an engineer, but I had no idea how my commerce peers thought about the world. I reached out to some economics professors and, long story short, I picked up an honors degree in finance/business. Building onto my engineering toolkit, I learned how accountants and economists think about the world. It was a great program. I learned a ton. But, most importantly, I learned that I didn't have to be an engineer.

ENGINEERING WAS JUST ONE TOOLKIT, BUT I HAD THE CORE THINKING TO EXPLORE MORE THAN THAT. AN IMPORTANT EARLY LESSON THAT, AS AN EXECUTIVE, I APPRECIATE DAILY.

And that is how I found myself at McKinsey & Company.

In my final years at university, as I decided to trade in my steel-toe caps for brogues, I didn't know the difference between a retail store and a retail bank. I knew I wasn't going to be an engineer. But what else could I be? At this point, I serendipitously overheard a conversation in an elevator on campus along the lines of *"McKinsey—oooh! aaah!"* So, I decided to take a deeper look.

By the time I entered my first interview, I knew McKinsey was the place for me. And it wasn't long before I was on the other side of the interview table.

McKinsey has a culture. Out of all the consulting firms, from the big four to the "top-tier MBB[1]" firms, I reckon McKinsey is the most institutionalized. Deeply engrained in their culture is that no matter where you are as a client—Paris, Houston, Jakarta—when you hire McKinsey consultants, you will get the McKinsey experience.

---

[1]   McKinsey; Bain and Boston Consulting Group

McKinsey not only prides itself on its multicultural fluidity, but it is also a core part of the operating model. Being able to ship in a luxury retail expert from Europe to work on a potential acquisition in Australia is key to McKinsey bringing the best to their clients. That's all well and good for the client. But it means that you must form multicultural teams, in a matter of days, for high-intensity strategy projects spanning anything from 3 to 12 weeks.

THESE STRATEGY CONSULTING TEAMS NEED TO HIT THE GROUND RUNNING ON VERY COMPLEX PROBLEMS.

Institutionalizing the McKinsey way of working and thinking is critical for that to work.

Once I had some time under my belt, I got involved in firm learning. I really liked coaching people—connecting with new and less-tenured consultants and helping them join some dots. What started out as giving modeling-skills training moved on to teaching problem-solving skills, communication and facilitation skills and eventually becoming global faculty on international training programs.

After four years, an interesting opportunity within McKinsey presented itself: an internal productivity initiative to codify and disseminate global engagement management best practices. It was a great experience and a very different view of how the firm thought and operated.

During my time at the firm, I received an incredible baptism into how business works. I would highly recommend a stint in top-tier consulting to anybody starting a career.

I left McKinsey and went into running and co-founding startups. I didn't want to trade in my consulting pain for the pain of working in large corporates. Thankfully, an opportunity to join a startup and head-up operations landed on my desk at the perfect moment. Co-founded by a couple of McKinsey alumni, an investment banker and a doctor, this profit-with-purpose B2C financial services venture wasn't growing fast enough. I fixed that.

I had found my niche. Startups offer the unique intersection of strategy, management responsibility, and a high degree of personal impact. And, as it turned out, I was pretty good at developing strategy in the boardroom and building high-performing teams to take that strategy into the world and make things happen.

ONE OF THE KEY THINGS I TOOK WITH ME INTO MY FIRST OPERATIONAL MANAGEMENT ROLE WAS "CONSULTANT THINKING."

We were a young, fast-moving organization. I hired youthful, dynamic people with good values, great intrinsic skills and the potential to grow quickly. Needing to rapidly develop a variety of skills, I reached out to my mates in other organizations and got referrals to training providers and programs. I set up discussions and did my due diligence.

THE PROBLEM WAS IT WAS ALL THE SAME: SIMILAR BASIC TRAINING DRESSED UP IN DIFFERENT BRANDING.

"Don't have a meeting if you can send an email" kind of thing. I had seen more, and I needed more. Hell, my managers deserved more.

So, I built my own tailored training, based on the skills I had learned and taught in consulting—but applying them to operational management challenges. Again, I was in a position to both build engaging training for the classroom and work with my managers to apply the concepts to the work they were doing. To really "get it and embed it." It was awesome and my managers (now lifelong friends) still rave about the advanced concepts they learned in those formative years.

On the back of a dynamic and capable management team, we scaled rapidly, re-engineered the business, survived our building burning down, and won multiple amazing awards. Startup one then turned into startup two, which turned into startup three: from life insurance, to new car sales, to legal technology. It has been amazing to work in such different industries, with such different people, blazing new trails.

Having built my third startup management team and seeing them settle into their roles, I was once again on the hunt for good management training. And, for the third time, my search for good management training left me empty handed.

Strike three. It was time to think bigger.

So, here we are. The ideas and concepts I present to you, and all the management programs I have developed, bring together four key ingredients:

Thought and Collaboration Leadership and Strategic Thinking from my consulting, faculty and internal-consulting experience in one of the world's most distinguished consulting firms.

Advanced Management Practices and Inspirational Leadership from being a COO and building my own high-performance management teams using some of these ideas and augmenting them with real world needs and experience.

Working with Executives and Managers as an independent consultant, advisor and non-Executive Director. And counselling friends over glasses of wine who have, themselves, progressed up and built, great organizations.

Observing Executives and Managers get it wrong. I've watched good and bad leaders leave significant personal and business opportunities on the table. They are either unaware of a key perspective that could unlock this potential for them or are simply too lazy to do the work to develop themselves and their Executive Operating Model.

Management is complex. As are people. I've structured this book in such a way that ideas and concepts build on one another to provide a more refined flavor than presenting discrete frameworks and tools.

Read it end-to-end to enjoy the full five course meal. Or, skip to the course that most satisfies your current craving.

SETTING THE SCENE: HOW MANAGEMENT COMPLEXITY HAS INCREASED
IN RECENT YEARS, WHILE MANAGEMENT DEVELOPMENT HAS BECOME
OVER-SIMPLIFIED.

We start by taking a quick look at the evolving world of management. I highlight some relevant reflections on how our management operating environment has changed from what it was 20 years ago and how the manager's role has become exceedingly more complex than it was before the internet, millennials and Covid.

We look at the 3Es of management development—Experience, Exposure and Education—and consider how we can more effectively tackle these to address the Dunning-Kruger effect; helping our managers overcome Mount Ignorant and accelerate their ascent up the Slope of Enlightenment.

THE EXECUTIVE MINDSET

Here we start to appreciate the day in the life of an executive. How does the world change from department and intermediate management to being in the C-Suite? We take a short tour of the various roles of an executive, so we are on the same page as them, and peek at some of the surprising things that keep them up at night. We then synthesize our learnings into the spheres of executive thinking and introduce the 5S Model.

THE 5S MODEL OF EXECUTIVE THINKING

To unpack the Five Core Spheres of the Executive Mindset, I have packaged this section into five different perspectives and mindsets that make up core executive thinking. While they work as a powerful ecosystem, we start with self, and we end in style.

- Manage Self
- Manage Strategy

- Manage Staff
- Manage Synergy
- Manage Style

Finally, we wrap up with some reflections on what makes a good executive great.

WARNING: There is no shortcut or framework that will turn someone into an executive overnight. Yes, there are some key elements that we will package together for easy reference, however, if you want to really accelerate a path to executive, the big drivers lie in on-the-job processes. As we explore how executives are made, reflect on how you can apply these principles in your everyday career. How can you be better apprenticed by your senior manager or executive? Do you have your own "up-or-out" policy? I will tie a lot together as we explore the 5S Model of Executive Thinking. And, as you will see in our problem-solving section:

YOU NEED TO ALLOW YOURSELF TIME TO DIVERGE AND THEN CONVERGE.

Explore. Reflect. Trial. Learn. Iterate. Development is an agile process.

And, if any of my prior staff, managers, colleagues or clients recognize the stories herein, thank you for the learnings you've given me and the opportunity for us to pass them on.

UNDER NEW MANAGEMENT

THE CHANGE WE HAVE SEEN IN THE WORLD OVER THE PAST 20 YEARS IS ASTRONOMICAL.

If you rewind and consider the worldly knowledge of the average manager before the internet became mainstream, it would be astonishingly low. This was only 25 years ago.

Studying, reading books, and so on was done in a specific field. You weren't bombarded all day, every day, by information across infinite topics: articles, news, blogs, book summaries, podcasts and so on. We are in an age where the tools are at our fingertips. You don't have to go to school or do an MBA to get access to the frameworks and models. There are literally thousands of articles and books online to give you that same content.

With this acceleration in global thinking and technology, we have seen an acceleration in the challenges on the manager's desk. Here is just a handful of reflections:

The knowledge explosion: School leavers and graduates simply know more. The manager is no longer managing a handful of thinkers and a sea of administrators. The move to paperless workplaces has both sped up and streamlined processes. The manager is no longer the smartest person in the room. Knowledge no longer correlates with experience.

The technology explosion: Artificial Intelligence (AI) is only a very small part of this. Pressure is on every department in every corner of the business to keep up with competition, and technology is key to driving productivity and efficiency. There are niche software systems for every need in every industry. Hundreds of them. And they are constantly changing and upgrading. Where we used to talk about agile software development and project implementation, we are now running agile cultures where change happens daily.

Diversity and inclusion: People have become more complicated. Minority rights, gender equality, identity proliferation: empathy, political correctness and language are taking up a lot more mental attention.

Remote work: Figuring out how to manage people without being in an office with them was a big challenge for most managers through the lengthy pandemic. Managing the aftermath of this—with staff recognizing and (not) appreciating the peripheral sacrifices they were making to go into the office—has put a lot of management teams on the back foot. Implementing new ways of working to cater for being offsite was hurried and remains new. Managing cabin fever was and remains challenging. Conversely, there is a new need to manage social anxiety—the lack of social resilience from months (years?) of not having to put up with a colleague sniffing for eight hours in the cubicle next to you. Mental health, fatigue, quiet quitting: these are all new topics on the management agenda that weren't labeled or talked about a decade ago.

De-centralized complexity: How do we centrally manage our fast-moving strategies and competitive advantage across infinitely more complex products, customer segments, sales channels, geographical cultures and internal cultures? We can't. We must decentralize complexity. And by that we mean that we centrally subscribe to a direction and a set of standards, but we must let our functions, regions, operations and support teams customize our ways of working to be both relevant and effective. Intermediate managers are the leaders carrying those torches.

Taking stock, the role of the intermediate manager is a complex one. The modern intermediate manager can be considered more of an orchestrator or conductor than a traditional manager.

AS WE STAND, THE COMPLEXITY OF THE ROLE OF THE INTERMEDIATE MANAGER CAN QUITE EASILY BE LIKENED TO THAT OF AN EXECUTIVE JUST 20 YEARS AGO.

As we turn our attention to how we are empowering our managers to deal with this new, complex world, I want to introduce the Dunning-Kruger effect. A lot of what we are doing isn't addressing this effect and may be making it worse.

BEWARE: THE DUNNING-KRUGER EFFECT

Graduates are smarter than ever and have all the world's knowledge at their fingertips. Yet our people are still desperately looking for good management training. Our response? We have resorted to "canning" learning into bite-sized chunks on prolific self-service platforms. We are over-simplifying a complicated ecosystem of skills—either because we think they will figure it out themselves or because we haven't taken the time to understand and distill them.

In "canning" management into a set of processes and tools for roll out—how to run a one-on-one, mechanical listening skills, "Ask questions to coach", and so forth—we run the risk of exacerbating the Dunning-Kruger effect.

The Dunning-Kruger2[2] effect is a psychological phenomenon where people with little knowledge or skill in a particular area believe they know more or are more skilled than they actually are. Essentially, it's when a little bit of knowledge leads a person to overestimate their abilities. Think "Google doctor."

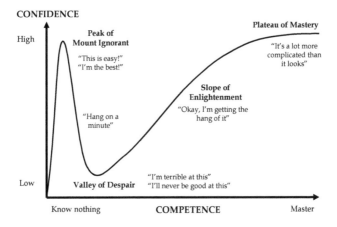

Chef Tom has just learned how to make an omelet. He's made it a few times at home, and it turned out pretty good. Feeling confident, Chef Tom decides to enter a cooking competition. He thinks, "I've got this, making an omelet is easy, and mine are great!" However, when he gets to the competition, he's surrounded by chefs making dishes with techniques and ingredients he's never seen before. Despite his initial confidence, Chef Tom quickly realizes that cooking is much more complex than he thought, and his simple omelet doesn't quite stack up. This is the Dunning-Kruger effect in action: Chef Tom initially overestimated his cooking skills because he didn't understand

---

[2]   https://mantracare.org/therapy/what-is/dunning-kruger-graph

the full scope of culinary arts. As he learned more and saw others' expertise, he began to recognize his own limitations.

Toolkits without experiential-thinking create a false sense of comfort and drive our managers up the peak of Mount Ignorant. Once the training wheels are off, they slide down the other side and into the Valley of Despair. No one told them it was coming. And no one has told them that they can only think their way out, not toolkit their way out.

Education without exposure without experience can leave your managers at the top of Mt Ignorant for longer than is necessary.

THE 3ES – EXPERIENCE, EXPOSURE AND EDUCATION

I professionally grew up in a world where development and learning were ingrained in the way you worked. I'm discussing this so that you can take these insights and incorporate them both into your own learning journey using my 5S Model (coming soon), and how you develop your managers and teams.

EXECUTIVE MANAGERS TAKE FULL RESPONSIBILITY FOR THEIR OWN DEVELOPMENT.

Having said that, it is helpful for your business to provide a learning ecosystem to help you. Junior managers rely on this. However, executive managers influence and shape it to get the value they need.

Around 50 years in the making, the 3E framework provides a guideline for how we should think about professional development:

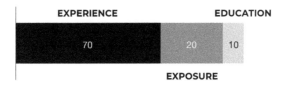

- **70% comes from Experience:** Doing things ourselves, day-to-day. Grappling with problems, opportunities and people in our daily work, within the context of our role and responsibilities.
- **20% comes from Exposure:** This is a bit more of an obscure bucket and I like to think of it as reactive versus proactive.

  - **Reactive exposure:** You are plodding along with a task or project, but you feel like you might be missing something or your boss isn't quite happy with the direction and results thus far. So, you hop online and start searching for examples. You hit up AI. You watch some YouTube videos. With a few more ideas and perspectives, you reach out to one of your senior colleagues and set up a working session so they can help you pull it all together.

  - **Proactive exposure:** You have never had to put a strategy together before. And it doesn't look like you will need to in the foreseeable future. I, however, am busy working on a strategy for a new service line. Seeing this as an opportunity for your development, to give you exposure to the process in the context of our actual work, I pull you in. You're pretty much a spectator, contributing thoughts and ideas here and there, but you don't have to contribute—you're there to be a sponge and soak up some new frameworks and perspectives.

- **10% comes from Education:** This is short, sharp, intensive immersion in theory, frameworks and case studies.

The potential problem with the application of this model is that many businesses, managers, and learning & development personnel view these three buckets as mutually exclusive.

You get given classroom training. It is totally unrelated to what you are doing on Monday. And those frameworks are unknown to your boss who doesn't use that approach or language.

Reactive exposure is equally inefficient. You don't know what you don't know. While you are spending weeks fumbling around with a challenging new project, there may be a colleague in the department next door who worked through something similar six months ago and could have saved you hours of wasted time and frustration. If only the leadership team were joining these dots.

It's not all doom and gloom. The "so what" of all of this is two-fold:

- The more you can collapse the 3Es — doing all three at the same time – the more effective the time (and money) spent will be and the faster you will learn.
- You need to take responsibility for your 3Es. Join the dots yourself. Find the Education facets that will help you now. Shape your Exposure ecosystem. And accelerate your Experience.

THE ISSUE WITH THE CURRENT SELF-SERVICE MANAGEMENT DEVELOPMENT PHENOMENON

Some of the mindsets and approaches I am seeing out there include:

Self-service: We are signing up for large scale, on-demand, virtual platforms. We are prioritizing quantity over quality. *Tom wants the freedom to choose. Tom knows what he wants to learn. I'm sure Tom will find something.* These platforms are scalable and cheap but Tom doesn't do any of what they offer. Tom could have found this stuff on the internet anyway.

Self-structured: *Each manager is unique and has their own needs so we will let them choose what to do.* First, managers don't know what they don't know. And second, if we are all learning different concepts, we can't work together using common concepts.

Unique: Tom heads up the support division so he has different needs to the VP of sales, so they need different training. Hard skills and tools that are silo-specific, maybe, but executive thinking skills are universal across the silos.

Annoying accountability: *We can track what Tom is doing on the back end. We will nag Tom's boss to make sure Tom is doing training.* Either Tom's boss doesn't care, or Tom starts ticking boxes by playing training videos in the background.

Low cohesion with no "ah-ha" factor: All of this leads to a disjointed, unexciting and unimpactful approach to management development. Training ends up being something on the internet that relates very randomly and lightly to what Tom is doing tomorrow. And no one is helping Tom join the dots or apprenticing Tom in the concepts to elicit true pupil-dilating "ah-ha!" moments.

> "I SIGNED MYSELF UP FOR AN ONLINE, ON-DEMAND STANDFORD PROGRAM. I DID TWO OF THE SESSIONS AND THEN THINGS GOT IN THE WAY AND MY MOTIVATION FIZZLED OUT. LIKE A NEW YEAR GYM MEMBERSHIP – I WAS KEEN. IT WAS AT MY FINGERTIPS. I SIGNED UP. AS EASY AS IT WAS TO SIGN UP – IT WAS EQUALLY EASY TO CHECK OUT."
>
> – SENIOR VICE PRESIDENT OF A TECH COMPANY

From the outside, it feels like intermediate management development is stuck. I believe we are over-simplifying and under-investing in intermediate management development. And one of the key reasons is that we leave it up to professional development departments to figure out education while relying on online management to figure out exposure and experience. It's inefficient and there is a better way.

> WE NEED TO TURN TRADITIONAL MANAGEMENT DEVELOPMENT ON ITS HEAD. WE NEED TO STOP THE REPETITIVE MONOLOGUE OF MECHANICAL TOOLS AND METAVERSES OF ON-DEMAND TRAINING THAT NO ONE USES. WE NEED TO START THE CONVERSATION ON COLLAPSING THE 3ES WITH ALL OUR PEOPLE LEADERS TO MAKE EVERY STRATEGIC TASK A DEVELOPMENT OPPORTUNITY. AND WE NEED TO DO ALL OF THIS IN A STRUCTURED WAY – AROUND A RELEVANT FRAMEWORK THAT TRANSCENDS PORTFOLIOS AND INDUSTRIES.

THE EXECUTIVE MINDSET

As we consider closing the gap between intermediate manager and executive, it's helpful to spend some time talking about the other side of the Valley of Despair.

As you ascend the corporate ladder, some things become easier, and some things become harder. As an example: Where, in the past, you were up against silo mentality and dealing with "Colin from Accounts" you now have a cross-silo view of the world. But you now have the responsibility to directly deal with the issue of Colin from Accounts. With the cross-silo view comes cross-silo responsibilities.

The perspectives and intricacies of any executive's role would be impossible to map out. So, I wanted to take an executive approach and share with you some of my reflections of where the world of the executive feels quite different to the world of a manager. To share perspectives.

We will start by appreciating how the unknown can often lead us to underestimate what it takes to succeed.

We will look at how experience changes the emotional attachment one has with the high and lows of the professional rollercoaster.

Then we take stock of the multitude of demands placed on the executive, who has limited resources and organizational attention to work with.

We understand the growing number of senior stakeholders an executive must manage and how the goal posts get moved by these stakeholders and influencers at an alarming rate.

And, last, we look at how, even though senior stakeholders and team members abound, the job of an executive is a very exposed and lonely one.

This sets us up well to introduce the 5S Model of Executive Thinking.

AN INSIDER'S GUIDE TO THE EXECUTIVE REALITY

The world of an executive is a complex one. As teenagers, we over simplify adulthood and adult responsibility, only to get a rude awakening when we eventually get to the adult table. I've seen the same reaction when people reach the boardroom.

Here, I want to take a walk through various aspects of what keeps an executive up at night, to give you insights into life at the professional adult table.

The Pete Factor

I've noticed that good executives have acquired what I like to call the "Pete Factor." I call it the Pete Factor because I worked with two different CEOs—both named Pete—that have embodied some executive qualities that money can't buy.

> *The first Pete was the CEO of a large investment firm and the chairman of a board of which I was part, in an executive capacity. Pete 1 was an all-round "nice guy." He had an air of stoicism about him, but he always weighed in when needed and had a thread of practicality around his strategic views and reasoning. As an executive, practical board input is always valued over theoretical bright ideas.*

As in any and all scale-up environments, the business and the board went through its ups and downs. It was during one of the particularly low lows that I had a coffee with Pete to chat about things and my impending breaking point.

Pete was so chilled. And the more chilled Pete was, the more frustrated I got (internally). Thoughts like "How can he not see how critical this is?" "Why isn't he freaking out—doesn't he care?" and "Either he isn't getting it or he doesn't care about helping me."

One thing led to another. That chapter passed and another one started.

Let me say that again: One thing led to another. That chapter passed and another one started.

Pete had seen this shit before—in endless shapes and sizes. Pete knew what he could control and what he couldn't. He also knew that I was freaking out like my world was going to end, the same way he may have when he was also early on in his career. But now, decades later, he had seen lots of complicated stuff—some far more complicated than what we were facing. Furthermore, Pete's firm had a number of investments: past, present and future. Some you win and some you don't. No matter how stressed out you get, the world keeps spinning.

I WAS ALL CONSUMED BY WHAT WAS MAYBE 5% OF PETE'S OVERALL AGENDA.

And while I wish Pete had made more of an effort to explain some of that to me, a large part of his emotional perspective and resilience came from having survived this shit many times before.

The second Pete was the CEO of a multi-national medical company. While different in stature, he was almost identical to Pete 1 in demeanor. Everyone in the company loved Pete. He was gentle, always smiling, and often ended sentences with a laugh.

Pete was also a savvy negotiator. In expanding into other countries, we often spoke about his engagements and negotiations with large healthcare

*providers that made exorbitant profits—mostly made through high con-
sumer prices and by screwing their suppliers—of which, Pete was going
to be a big one.*

*Pete was CEO of a medical company. Doctors and nurses are notoriously
difficult to manage. Doctors because they are doctors. And nurses because
they have to work in extremely challenging environments and report to
doctors.*

*Pete was somehow managing all of this—but still had the perspective and
self-management to joke with the nurses when visiting a clinic and be
an inspirational leader both internally and externally, as the face of the
company.*

The second Pete had an equally measured view of the world and didn't
allow the demands of the job to let him lose emotional perspective.

I can't help but think about the number of times, early on in my
career, that I thought: *This is so complicated, why are they being so calm?*

Or, conversely, *why are they making it so complicated?* The answer is
so simple.

The reality is that in executive matters, I had a very limited view of
all the balls in the air. I was quite naïve looking at the situations from
Mt Ignorant.

The more experienced I have become, the more I have realized how
complicated the world really is.

Welcome to the Plateau of Mastery.

Fast forward a couple of years and I've had some Pete Factor situations
of my own. And I have chosen to handle them slightly differently.

*In one instance, the startup I was leading entered a(nother) perfect storm:
we were trying to raise capital, the global economy was struggling, the market
wanted our product and we had run into some core scalability issues. The
team was overwhelmed and very anxious about our ability to make it through.*

In one particular meeting with one of my managers, they turned to me and said, "How can you be so Zen at a time like this?!"

I knew then and there that I had become a Pete. And I knew I owed it to my manager to explain why I was so Zen.

First, I wasn't Zen. Inside I was angry, frustrated, anxious, exhausted... But, if I showed all of that, it would have totally killed the team emotionally. It was my job to keep it together and figure shit out. Secondly, I had seen this shit before. This wasn't the first time I was faced with diminishing runway and scalability issues. In one of my prior startups, we got to a point where we realized the business model was fundamentally not going to work. And, again, we would figure stuff out. And, if we didn't, we would close the company, like thousands had done before. It's not desirable and certainly not part of the plan. But you win some and you lose some. And I had been around long enough to know quite a few people whose startups didn't make it. No one died. And they went on to do other cool stuff. All of this added to my Pete Factor account. Understanding my manager's pain and frustration, I explained all of this to them.

I HAD THE EXECUTIVE MANAGER CONVERSATION.

I took the time to explain the bigger picture and allow them inside the mind of an executive.

I GAVE THEM EXPOSURE TO SOME PETE FACTOR, DIRECTLY LINKED TO RECENT *EXPERIENCE.*

Pete Factor is actually equal parts perspective and equal parts **self-management**. Both Pete's had infinitely more stressors than I did, with infinitely higher stakes. But they managed those stressors like an executive: show up with a smile, ready to inspire.

Executives are (generally) not idiots

Executives generally know what is wrong in their business. Good executives know what is worth worrying about and what is worth fixing. We will chat about heatmapping in the 5S Model. This is a very useful exercise and something that good executives do unconsciously.

> *I will never forget the first time I was faced with consultants after I had left consulting. The CEO at the time had set up a meeting with a bunch of consultants who were purported to be "call center gurus." I politely went along and listened to their pitch and credentials and what not. They knew what they were talking about and had good experience and credentials.*

> *When debriefing, I said to the CEO, "You realize we will pay these guys thousands of dollars to come in and tell us everything we already know that is wrong with our business?"*

That list was not short. It never is. Entrepreneurs have no shortage of ideas, what they lack is the time, money and resources to make all those ideas a reality. Good executives have no shortage of issues and opportunities. What they lack is the time, money and resources to address them.

The targets are always moving

As the sayings go: "change is the only constant" and "time flies." The demands of business at the higher levels are constantly changing and changing fast. Changes in product, customer demands, the market and economy, competitors, whatever—these all have ripple effects through the business.

And there is no sheet music for this symphony. Executives must write and re-write the music for all the sections as they go along.

The strategy you have just seen looks great. Simple and elegant. The executive team has worked on this, behind the scenes, with myriad stakeholders, for months. With all the stakeholders at play, the strategic balls in the air are vast.

> **THE EXECUTIVE'S JOB IS TO KEEP THEIR EYES ON THE BALLS; IF THEY ARE GOING TO DROP ONE, BEFORE THAT HAPPENS THEY MUST DECIDE WHICH ONE TO DROP AND HOW TO PICK UP THE PIECES.**

Boards and executives review strategies regularly; frequently more often than they should. In larger corporates, with different executives in a weird array of matrix reporting structures, there is always someone doing a strategic review. This puts pressure on the entire system. It asks some questions that need answering and asks many that don't.

Welcome to corporate politics.

Good executives know how to **manage strategy** and what needs focus and resources.

People management becomes infinitely more complex the higher you get in any organization

An intermediate manager with three managers and, say, 30 people in their collective teams will face people, process and tech issues. If one of the staff is having a challenge with a particular project/client/target, their manager helps them and if it's significant enough, you will get called in to assist. Now, the role of the person having the challenge or the job that you are rallying around is still relatively simple. It's easy to map outcomes and process and a lot of the work is linear in nature.

As you move up the people pyramid, jobs become complicated. There are linear and non-linear issues. Managers' jobs are complex. Showing that a poorly performing manager isn't performing is extremely difficult. Trying to figure out what isn't working with a more senior manager and their portfolio is all the more complicated.

THE ABSTRACT NATURE OF THE PROBLEMS YOU FACE MULTIPLY AT AN
EXPONENTIAL RATE.

And when you have 500 people under your portfolio, the chances of a
materially complicated and very high-risk issue popping up, that needs
your urgent attention, is extremely high. Often multiples of these pop
up at a given time and generally it happens right before a holiday period
when no one has the energy to deal with it.

For an executive to manage all this proactively and reactively, they
need both well-developed analytical and abstract reasoning, along with
substantial emotional resilience as they support and/or fight people
through these problem-solving processes.

I have had to deal with and sort out a frightening amount of weird
shit that my management teams have had absolutely no idea about, for
the sake of their faith in leadership and the broader company culture.
Weird shit with very high stakes for the business at large.

Good executives know that weird shit is coming. They don't know
when and they don't know where from, so, they do their best to be
proactively prepared to deal with it in the most painless way possible.

Great executives **manage staff** across multiple portfolios and departments to get things done and keep people happy.

Executives have a lot of stakeholders at play

Following on from the above, I have alluded to the myriad stakeholders
that an executive needs to engage with and manage. The intermediate
manager typically sees only the internal stakeholders and teams.

The first big change at senior leadership/executive level is the inher-
itance of a second team—**the executive team**. Executive teams are a
team unto themselves. While each has their own portfolio of responsibility, everyone engages on business-wide strategies and issues. This is
possibly one of the biggest shifts I see in people moving from middle
to senior management.

Managers spend so long focusing on mastering their department or function as they deal with management impostor syndrome. Once they have a semblance of control and mastery, they stay in their lane, and protect their turf. They are careful not to throw trash into other people yards, for fear that their yard gets trashed or placed under scrutiny.

Having built up self-confidence over the years by being knowledgeable about a space and how it works, it's difficult for managers to let go of that and engage in other people's portfolios. Over and above giving meaningful opinions and input about other people's portfolios, there is the eventual realization that all portfolios are collectively owned by the executive. They all must work in tandem to deliver value. And that is what executives are ultimately responsible for.

> **GREAT EXECUTIVES HAVE TO DELIBERATELY ORCHESTRATE HOW PORTFOLIOS WORK, OR DON'T WORK TOGETHER.**

The second new stakeholder group is **business partners**. At an executive level, you are supposed to seek out useful partners (formal and informal). These may be business partners to boost go-to-market strategies. These may be friends who are senior leaders in other businesses who meet regularly to exchange ideas. Then there is the barrage of consultants trying to sell you insights, projects, and systems. A lot of mental bandwidth is spent engaging with and navigating this.

The third stakeholder group is the **board and shareholders**.

Every boss has a boss. The CEO's boss is the board and the board's boss is the shareholder. Shareholders report to their bank managers. And so, the world turns.

A surprising amount of time goes into managing external board members and shareholders. They all have a vested interest in the business's success. Apart from formal board and shareholder meetings, there is a lot of peripheral engagement in one-on-ones, risk, remuneration and finance committee meetings, and ad hoc discussions with the group and its members. Boards and shareholders are also given reports and other formal and informal communications.

All this takes time. Even in large corporates with departments set up solely for this purpose, they can't magically come up with board messaging and strategies without significant input from executives and the executive team.

All these stakeholder groups come with personalities, opportunities, issues and challenges.

Great executives need to **manage synergy** between myriad internal and external stakeholders to deliver maximum value.

And that brings me to our last peek inside the executive mind.

The executive's job is a lonely one

It's tough at the top. The higher you get, the lonelier it gets.

So, I am going to add:

> THE MORE EXPERIENCED I HAVE BECOME, THE MORE I HAVE REALIZED HOW COMPLICATED THE WORLD REALLY IS.
>
> AND THE MORE I LEARN THAT NOBODY HAS THEIR SHIT FIGURED OUT.

I have yet to work with a C-Suite executive who thinks they are good at their job or can say with confidence *I know what I'm doing*. This reminds me of one of my strangest situations as a young consultant:

It was dark, around 8pm, and I thought I was the only person left on that floor of our client's massive high-rise building. Out of the corner of my eye, I noticed some lights flicker on—triggered by energy saving motion sensors—and our lead client came walking over. Maybe late-40s, early-50s, she pulled up a chair, sat down and burst into tears.

This was my second project in consulting, and this was not covered in any of my training. The pressure of the transformation strategy, the disgruntlement in her flailing team and her shouldering all the responsibility to make this work was becoming all too much. And she had no one to talk to.

She couldn't talk to her COO or CEO for fear of appearing weak and out of her depth. Talking to coaches or advisers removed from the business was pointless because they didn't have enough context to be practically useful or have real empathy. Talking to the McKinsey seniors or partners was both intimidating and could result in them reporting back to the CEO that she wasn't going to cut it.

So, at 8pm on a Tuesday night, she chose my shoulder to cry on. And I'm glad I was there to help. That wasn't the last executive breakdown I have witnessed firsthand, but at 26 years old, it gave me a lot of insight and compassion for the loneliness of the executive's job.

It's tough at the top. All eyes are on you, especially in the tough times, to manage yourself, manage strategy, manage staff and manage synergy across functions and stakeholders. And, you have to do all this with inspiration and gravitas. Great executives **manage style** to be inspirational leaders and create followership.

As you can see, great executives manage a complex set of facets and perspectives, spanning multiple time horizons by using their ability to:

- Manage self
- Manage strategy
- Manage staff
- Manage synergy
- Manage style

Welcome to the 5S Model of Executive Thinking.

WHAT IS THE EXECUTIVE MINDSET?

As you take control of your own development and work on collapsing education, exposure and experience, the 5Ss of executive thinking should be your focus areas. So, as we begin to explore the 5S Model of Executive Thinking in detail, I want to capture here a synthesis of the characteristics of a great executive. The 5S Model will help you to start incorporating executive thinking into your current role and responsibilities, but it is helpful to know where you are going.

> **UNCOVERING THE EXECUTIVE TOOLKIT IS THE MISSION. EXECUTIVE THINKING IS THE VISION.**

Great executives **manage SELF**. They:

- build authentic trust quickly and effectively by knowing their core characteristics; owning how and when these can be destructive.
- set themselves up in the right roles and ecosystems to play to those strengths—focusing on long-term success for themselves and the business, not faking it till you make it.
- have a compelling leadership story and know what's next for them and their people.

Great executives **manage STRATEGY**. They:

- join the dots between company strategy, functional strategies and departmental strategies, with a compelling narrative about how the company got here and what they need to focus on.
- think "what's next?" and don't wait for things to happen—they get stuff done. The right stuff.
- are thought leaders AND problem-solving leaders—if they don't know the answer, they coordinate structured efforts to find the answer.

Great executives **manage STAFF**. They:

- are the custodians of their portfolio's vision, mission and values.
- build effective high-performance teams with the right mix of smarts, culture and personality types, facilitating compelling career journeys for their high performers.
- manage from the balcony and in the dance, on the stage and behind the stage, to effectively focus the limited resources of energy, attention and resilience in the long-term game.

Great executives **manage SYNERGY**. They:

- also manage their exec team by joining the dots across portfolios to drive business synergy.
- are great influencers, seeing org chart lines for what they are.
- are masters of collaboration that targets both hearts and minds to make working together meaningful and memorable.

Great executives **manage STYLE**. They:

- understand their broader conscious and subconscious impact to have gravitas and inspire followership.
- are interesting.
- are clear and succinct; dynamic and engaging.

THE 5S MODEL OF EXECUTIVE THINKING

T he 5S Executive Thinking Model tackles the five different elements and mindsets a good intermediate manager should develop to up their game. This ecosystem of mindsets works in tandem that feed off one another to make an executive great. Any missing link hampers the other four components and risks the possibility of slipping back into the "good enough" bucket.

However, in *building up* these mindsets, there is a logical progression through the elements.

At the start we have **manage self**. Having a structured approach to understanding your intrinsic strengths and biases is critical in determining how you are naturally effective at the other elements. While the concept of "authentic leadership" comes to mind, we are going to tackle that for all its positives and negatives to make sure we are managing ourselves and not kidding ourselves.

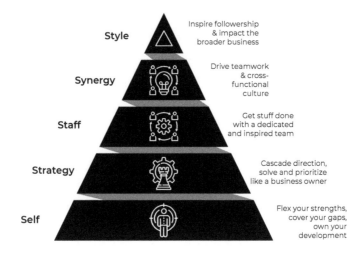

Second is **manage strategy**. A content-free leader is a useless leader. When the going gets tough and your team needs help, real impact and change can only come from helping the team cut through challenges and have a clear path forward. The problem-solving processes you drive, the emotional support you provide, the trade-offs you weigh up and priorities you focus on, all depend on the direction of travel and scenarios that may unfold. Thought leadership, problem solving and inspiring direction are at the core of great executive thinking.

Next is **manage staff**. By definition, a manager has people that they are responsible for. These direct responsibilities, and the structure that a solid line elicits, is our first step in managing other humans. Very few people do this well. And even fewer do this in a structured way that allows them to coach others on how to best manage their team. And, drawing off our **manage self** learnings, we can add advanced nuances to team management that supersede over-simplified, one-size-fits-all management tools.

The intermediate manager and executive has a second team with which they need to **manage synergy**. Managers are also responsible for managing their peers, cross-functional collaboration and executive teamwork. Beyond direct line reporting, we build on **manage self** and **manage strategy** with collaboration and influencing tools to more broadly impact the business and organizational levels.

Finally, we open our executive awareness to the organization and world at large and discuss the fifth element of **manage style**. Our professional style is the essence of our leadership model—an essence that affects those around us in many unconscious and indirect ways. Here, we unpack some of the facets of leadership style and how you can build your authentic leadership persona to elicit followership and have broader impact on the organization.

WORKING ON THE 5S ELEMENTS WILL MAKE YOU A BETTER MANAGER TOMORROW. MASTERING THEM WILL BUILD YOU INTO A GREAT EXECUTIVE THAT EVERYONE WANTS TO WORK FOR.

MANAGE SELF

"All progress starts with ruthless honesty about where you are. Self-deception only wastes time. Face reality and then change it."

−SCOTT D CLARY; ENTREPRENEUR, INVESTOR AND AUTHOR, HOST OF THE
SUCCESS STORY PODCAST, FOUNDER AND CEO OF THE SOCIAL CLUB

P eople are different. Your staff, your boss, the manager of accounts, your significant other—no matter how much you wish they thought like you do, they don't. Understanding yourself and how you differ from those around you is core to being an executive manager. But understanding is not enough. You need to lead others. You need to coach others.

You need to influence up, down and side-to-side. **Managing self** to manage others is proactive and tactical.

We will start by exploring trust and the concept of the emotional bank account—an eye-opening idea I was gifted early in my professional journey.

We will build on this with personality profiling frameworks to gain a deeper appreciation of the different ways people build trust and how your authentic self could destroy trust. We will look to synthesize this into a couple of core leadership styles for you to work with.

We look at 360-degree feedback as a key tool for understanding how you are **managing self** across your known characteristics and look into some surprises that may pop up. I provide some key questions to ask and how to think about synthesis.

We then roll this into a broader inspirational leadership story and consider what your next chapter could look like. While useful when recruiting and onboarding new team members, reflecting on your journey and what has influenced your leadership style can uncover valuable stories to weave into your coaching and apprenticeship toolkit.

Finally, we do the hard work. We develop your management heatmap. We map out how your core characteristics work as a strength or as a weakness in the context of your role and responsibilities. We consider structural ways to shore up those characteristics, to cover blind spots and mitigate trust leakage.

Straight out of the gates, let me make one of my biggest management principles very clear:

PEOPLE DON'T CHANGE.

The sooner you appreciate this fact, the more effective you will be in all areas of life.

Yes, people gain self-awareness and evolve. I am a far less spikey person than I was 20 years ago. But I'm still spikey. I am a firm believer that the 80/20 of our core personality traits and talents are well developed somewhere in middle-childhood, between the ages of 6 and 12 years. This is when we grow our spikes. Often (not always) these spikes get filed down with adult independence—working in a world that isn't fair, for bosses who aren't fair, and having to clean your own kitchen. Accordingly, I term this first 5S element of executive thinking **manage self** and not lead self.

I am a decisive, skeptical, highly structured, macro thinker. I have been all my life. And no matter how much my wife tries to get me to "see the bright side", "just be positive" and not get angry with slow walkers. I am who I am, and I have not been able to change that. However, a skeptical arsehole may become a skeptical person, who may, in turn, become a skeptical executive. Their fundamental skeptical characteristic remains and denying that would be silly. (An interesting thought is whether the aim of psychology would be to study the source of my skepticism or to change my skepticism...?)

Either way, we **manage self**. We get a clearer view of self, and we understand self. We open Johari's Window[3]. We align the core characteristics that make us tick. We understand the good and the bad stuff and then we manage our role, our team and our management systems to cater for ourselves and be the executive we were born to be.

BUILDING TRUST AND EMOTIONAL BANK ACCOUNTS

Trust is the foundation of human interaction. No matter what you want to accomplish as a member of a team, let alone a leader, you must have the trust of your audience to have any impact on them. Equally important, having trust speeds up impact! By avoiding doubt, mitigating inefficient emotional journeys, and eliminating unnecessary objections, we can focus engagement on the real issues.

In the classic book *The Trusted Adviser*, David Maister et al presented

---

[3] Johari's Window is a psychological tool used to help people better understand their relationship with themselves and others. Created by Luft and Ingham in the 1950s, it is effectively a two-by-two matrix of "known/unknown to me" and "known/unknown to others." This gives four quadrants or "windows." The overall objective is to uncover the unknown unknowns to untapped potential and talents.

the trust equation. I'm presenting it here again, over 20 years later, as we will use it as a foundation to hang some advanced thinking on.

$$\text{Trust} = \frac{(\text{Credibility} + \text{Reliability} + \text{Intimacy})}{\text{Perception of Self-Orientation}}$$

Please read the book if you haven't. But, in a nutshell, you want to *add to the numerator* and *subtract from the denominator* to increase trust.

Adding to the numerator

Credibility: This relates somewhat to the words we speak. In a business context, it refers to the expertise or the perceived competence of the adviser. Having useful content, experience, and insights to contribute, gives you credibility. Qualifications, certifications, and relevant prior work experience adds to credibility.

Reliability: This relates to actions and emphasizes the importance of consistently delivering on promises and acting in a dependable manner. This covers physical actions like being on time, attending a meeting you accepted, meeting a deadline. More importantly, it also extends to consistency of values, opinions, narratives and acting in the objective and transparent best interests of a greater good.

Intimacy: This refers to the safety or security that one feels when entrusting someone with confidential information. Fundamentally, this means that I understand you, I care about you, and I have your back—so you can trust me to act in a way that won't harm you personally.

Subtracting from the denominator

Self-orientation or **perception of self-orientation**: This refers to the age-old question: What's in it for me? And in most high-pressure situations, there are several moving parts and high stakes on the outcome. Especially people's careers, job security, chances of a promotion, etc.

The adviser's focus and whether it is directed toward interests that are mutually beneficial or may be detrimental to the other person, is fundamental to the trust in the relationship. Remember: It doesn't matter if I know what you want, I agree with that, and I'm acting in accordance with that—but you doubt my intentions. *Perception of intent is as important as actual intent.*

Take a moment, at some point, to think about people in your life that you trust with your personal and professional life and do a quick reflection, using the equation, to see what stands out for each person.

Emotional bank account

One of the earliest nuggets I received from a McKinsey director was the idea of the "emotional bank account." He said:

> "IF YOU WANT TO MAKE A WITHDRAWAL OUT OF THE EMOTIONAL BANK ACCOUNT, YOU'RE BETTER OFF HAVING A POSITIVE BALANCE TO BEGIN WITH."

Over the years, I have found more and more richness underlying this simple concept.

The emotional bank account is equal parts trust and contributions to the well-being and betterment of the other person.

Building the emotional bank account takes effort. You must be proactive and look for opportunities to make deposits into the account. Organically building a balance is time consuming and can be hit-and-miss. Especially for leaders who have responsibility and influence over people. Starting with support is far more effective than trying to battle doubt!

There will be withdrawals. In any high-performing business situation, there will be demands, there will be discomfort, shit will hit the fan. In these instances, having a healthy emotional bank account will not only get you through the storm, but it will also give you comrades who will hold the umbrella for you.

A good example of this is when I was working on an operational strategy for an industrial company. One of the key stakeholders was the people executive. I had built up broader trust through the project and she was a supporter of the overall project. Our mutual emotional bank account was fairly even and insignificant.

Through the project, I had noticed some challenges her team was facing interacting with some of the pricklier operations managers. I had seen this a hundred times before and I knew I had some thinking I could give to her that would help her and her team align around a clearer HR operating model and more effective boundaries.

I set up a working session centered around the operating strategy project and took her through the observations— focused on how I thought the role of her people business partners wasn't being properly appreciated and respected by some of the ops managers. I knew she knew this as we had discussed it in a broader project meeting. I walked her through a central-ization framework that clearly articulated and juxtaposed the different models—and we discussed the observation that some of the ops managers, coming from backgrounds of other operating models, were approaching this out of naivety and not malice.

Fast forward a couple of months and we were drafting a(nother) CEO newsletter together over a bottle of wine.

None of this had anything to do with the project directly, but it was a clear opportunity for the business and the people lead. She learned some stuff, had a thought partner to work with and kicked off some new impactful initiatives. She shone. WIIFM? (or "What's in it for me?") I love people strategy. A business strategy is only as good as the people strategy that delivers it. Working on this stuff is fun and rewarding. Fun and reward that balanced my attending shift-change meetings at 4:30 am in the middle of winter. My self-orientation aligned 100% with the people lead's needs (intimacy).

I had the credibility: experience (prior work), real observations in the business and the insightful framework to help. I acted reliably in that I didn't email her the framework and say, *have a nice day*. I met with her and discussed the framework and helped her think through an approach and next steps. I did the typing.

In a professional environment, we want to be building trust and an emotional bank account as quickly as possible.

> **IT'S CRITICAL TO APPRECIATE THAT DIFFERENT PERSONALITIES HAVE DIFFERENT PRIORITIES AND NEEDS ACROSS THE TRUST EQUATION!**

Trust isn't the same for everyone.

PERSONALITY AND LEADERSHIP PROFILES

John Verdon, in his book *Think of a Number*[44] , writes:

> *We each seem to be wired to believe* **my situation** *causes my problem, but* **your personality** *causes yours. My desire to have everything my way seems to make sense, while your desire to have everything your way seems infantile.*

Take a little time to think across the elements of the trust equation and reflect on how you like trust to be built with you. What do you deem to be credible? What kills reliability for you? How have people successfully built up intimacy with you in a professional environment? What does *your* personality need to trust another?

Now, think of your mother (or wife, or husband, or "side hustle"— someone you know pretty well). How does their trust equation work?

My wife is a die-hard Google doctor. Sadly, I know that if I have a heart attack, she will shove cayenne pepper in my mouth. Even though I don't have life insurance, that will probably put the nail in the coffin. Why? Because she saw it on some random Facebook reel, and she believed it. And remember, my wife is a lawyer.

---

4   Kindle edition. Page 106

> SO, PLEASE, DON'T MAKE THE ROOKIE MISTAKE OF THINKING THAT THE WAY *YOU* LIKE TRUST TO BE BUILT WITH YOU IS THE WAY OTHER PEOPLE LIKE TRUST TO BE BUILT WITH *THEM*.

Personalities come in a complex array of different shapes and sizes, and you need to have a deep and honest appreciation for that if you are going to be an effective executive manager.

Personality profiling

HR has killed the most valuable leadership tool I use daily—personality profiles. For 20 years, I have successfully used a wide variety of personality profiling frameworks, *as a manager and executive*, not as a coach. My belief is that these valuable frameworks have got a bad rap because of two issues.

First, large corporate HR departments with too much budget, and too little connection with line management, roll out canned personality tests to tick a box and celebrate success in their silos. Staff are emailed a link, they answer some questions, and they get a canned, glossy report. Some may get a couple of hours at an offsite with a highly qualified facilitator to stand in the pink quadrant and point at their colleagues in the azure quadrant. On Monday, it's business as usual. This light approach undermines the purpose and depth of the frameworks and makes them seem like they are no more useful than horoscopes. Which, with this approach, is true.

Second, they are used in personal transformation work. Many of the richer frameworks are used by coaches and psychologists as part of long-term coaching methodologies. This often involves deep introspection and an expectation of personal transformation and development. Most of my staff have not and will not sign up for that. Personal development, yes. Personal transformation and shadow work and the like, no.

It has become so bad that I am now seeing management development programs that explicitly market that they *don't* do personality profiling.

THE RESULT: PERSONALITY PROFILING FRAMEWORKS REMAIN A SECRET
WEAPON FOR EXECUTIVE MANAGERS WHO DIG DEEPER AND UNDERSTAND THE
TRUE ESSENCE THEY CAN BRING TO MANAGEMENT.

In my experience, personality profiling tools come in two flavors: behavior-based frameworks and motivation-based frameworks.

In management, we are most interested in motivation-based frameworks.

Behavior-based frameworks are very useful in getting teams to work together on the surface. How do people process information? What are their communication styles and preferences? Do they get energy from engaging with others or find it exhausting? These what and how questions can help us expedite the formation of team norms to drive effective team dynamics. We used the Myers Briggs framework very successfully at McKinsey.

If I am looking for insight into how to build trust with Tom, how to motivate Tom and how to influence Tom, I need to look at Tom's "why." And that's where motivation-based frameworks come in.

Motivation-based frameworks

These frameworks talk to the underlying personal needs, values and, hence, motivations underlying how people behave and interact with the world. Good frameworks also consider how self-aware or integrated someone is in their personality. The best frameworks *don't* pigeonhole someone into one of 4 or 9 or 16 boxes.

I use the Enneagram framework. I have been using it, as a manager and executive, for well over a decade. I took the time to get an advanced accreditation in using the framework. In my first startup, we had around ten accredited practitioners in the business. I have completed hundreds of assessments and walked the business world with these team members, managers and executives and seen the reflections of the Enneagram firsthand. The assessment methodology I use ranks an individual's core value system. I use this level of detail to broadly categorize personalities into around 250 different types.

There are a number of free resources online which are directionally useful[5]. But a thorough, in-depth assessment is always preferable. Here is a quick table of Enneagram energy descriptors and some of their associated values to give you a flavor.

#	ENERGY DESCRIPTOR	ASSOCIATED VALUES
1	Strict Perfectionist	To be right, logical consistency, honesty, self-discipline, morality, ethics, order, justice, conscience, self-control
2	Considerate Helper	To be appreciated, friendship, love, being needed, being helpful, faithfulness, altruism, friend-ship, community
3	Competitive Achiever	To be successful, achievement, goal oriented, success, good reputation, recognition, popularity (with those that matter)
4	Intense Creative	To be original, personal freedom, authenticity, originality, self-expression, creativity, aesthetic and artistic beauty, depth of feelings, connection
5	Quiet Specialist	To be competent, knowledge, efficiency, intelligence, logical reasoning, fact-oriented, originality of thought, understanding, perceptiveness
6	Loyal Skeptic	To be secure, responsibility, duty, cooperation, acceptance, persistence, hard work, commitment, duty, loyalty
7	Enthusiastic Visionary	To be happy, experience, sensual pleasure, amusement and excitement, variety, spontaneity, happiness, accomplishment
8	Active Controller	To be strong, independence, influence, control, power, physical survival, resources, wealth, respect of others, greatness
9	Adaptive Peacemaker	To be at peace, stability, unity, harmony, emotional well-being, routine, traditional values, acceptance of what is, peace

[5] **www.trueself.io** is pretty good for main type but not full Enneagram stacking.

The most important part is that *it works*. But you need to put in the investment to really understand the framework and marry it with good executive thinking to unlock its real potential.

So, why a framework at all? Surely everyone is an individual.

Agreed. Everyone is weird and wonderful in their own random way. A rich and accurate personality profiling framework, in the hands of a good practitioner, is a kick-starter. A personality profiling framework gives you a language and methodology for unpacking personality characteristics.

A GOOD FRAMEWORK HELPS YOU JUXTAPOSE PERSONALITY TRAITS SO YOU CAN APPRECIATE THE AUTHENTICITY OF OTHERS, HOW THEY DIFFER FROM YOU, AND WHAT THEY NEED FROM YOU AS A MANAGER.

Any framework you have access to is better than no framework. Having a common language and starting point to assess and review your person-ality characteristics, and how they may be similar or different to those you lead and work closely with, is at the crux of the matter. However, you need to make it a working framework. This is not an interesting, once-off HR exercise. This is a management tool that you can refer to and use every single day. And it starts with you.

Core to (good) personality profiling frameworks is the concept of characteristics. This is important as it is a significant departure from strengths and weaknesses.

I was once asked in an interview: *Give us one of your strengths. And then give us a weakness.* I answered: *I'm decisive. And I'm decisive.* Obviously, one of my core characteristics is decisiveness. Depending on how I use it and the context, it can be a strength, or it can be a weakness. Knowing I am decisive, I need to **self manage** this characteristic so that I don't bulldoze the team who are still making up their minds; don't jump into action and leave people behind; don't make a hasty decision without assessing all the facts and consulting others for insight.

Using a good profiling tool to give you a hitlist of characteristics that could accurately describe you is the starting point. Taking that list and determining what is accurate and how you are managing these characteristics is key.

360-degree feedback

Now, no surprise, your judgment of your characteristics is only mildly accurate.

I've seen pretty polarizing reactions to personality profiling results: there are the characteristics where people say, *Wow, that read me like a book. I totally do x and y all the time.* Then there is the hesitancy around a couple of characteristics that *kinda don't resonate.*

I grin every time that someone says to me, *so, I asked my husband to read it. He laughed and agreed with everything!* The challenge is that maybe it isn't you. Or maybe you just don't know that it is you. Either way, you need to find out if you want to be an executive manager and you need to find out often.

360-degree feedback is an invaluable tool to start exploring your leadership profile. And it is quite simple. As we said earlier: Executives make shit happen, they don't wait for shit to happen. Don't go to HR and suggest instilling 360-degree feedback surveys into the HR calendar. Just put together a Google form and send it out.

What are we looking for? We are looking for succinct insight into how others see your core characteristics as a leader, how you are using them as a strength and where they may be showing up as a weakness. Depending on the situation, it may or may not be advantageous to make the feedback anonymous. Sometimes it is helpful to synthesize the input using the perspective that it was given from. However, some conflict-avoiding personality types tend to be more open and honest behind a veil.

When running structured 360-degree feedback, I run the following process:

- Same set of questions for all levels.
- Feedback givers provide their names.
- Everyone knows that the feedback will be given to the person being reviewed, word for word, BUT without the names of the people giving feedback.
- The names are used by me/the people department to help synthesize the overall outcomes and guide debrief conversations.

That way, if you get outlying feedback from poor performers that isn't helpful to the individual, you can help them navigate that.

What three words?

One of the most powerful questions you can ask your team, colleagues and seniors is: **What three words would you use to describe him/her?** I always start my 360-degree questionnaires with this question. It drives synthesis and prioritization. As above, it's useful to reflect on the trends in word themes, as well as the outliers:

- How do these words correlate with my personality type and leadership style?
- How do these words reinforce how I have deliberately tried to lead my team and peers over the period?
- Which of these words are consistent with past surveys?
- Which are new?
- Which are surprising?

The routine five questions I like to ask are:

1. What three words would you use to describe this team member?
2. What do their strongest allies say about them?
3. What do their harshest critics say about them?
4. How would you describe this person's leadership style?
5. How would you rate this person out of 10? What would they need to do to make them a 10/10?

And that's it. I try not to ask any other questions. This drives synthesis and focus, and, in my experience, brings out all the necessary feedback that is required.

Synthesizing the answers

It is critical when synthesizing the answers to account for the operating context the feedback was given in.

Random example 1: The economy sucks, the business has just had a restructure, it's the middle of winter, people are at an energy low and feel a bit betrayed by management. This will impact results and must be applied as a filter.

Random example 2: You've just taken over from another manager that everyone liked, but who was not driving performance. You have come in and are pushing buttons to get more focus and output and less buggering-around. Obviously, this will be reflected in the feedback.

What I look for is surprises.
If the feedback says I have been autocratic, but I have purposefully been autocratic for the good of the team and business—then fine, no surprise. If I have tried hard to be inclusive and a servant leader, and the feedback oozes "autocratic" then this would be an unpleasant surprise worth unpacking.

Coming back to trust

With deeper insight into your core motivations and characteristics, it is much easier to characterize how you naturally build trust and how you naturally trust others. Actions and evidence that align with your core motivations and characteristics as strengths make you trust people. Once you have done a personality profiling test that you are relatively happy with, go back to the trust equation and consider how you naturally build trust across the elements. Also consider how you can potentially diminish trust through your natural characteristics.

Now, shifting the focus to building trust with others: Can you appreciate that your natural propensity is to try and build trust with others *through your personality's lens?* The way you like to see credibility *in* others is the same way you will try and show credibility *to* others. The same goes for reliability, intimacy, and self-orientation.

This can be a total waste of time. Or, even worse, this can diminish trust!

Over the years, I have worked with many very smart individuals. I'm sure you have shared the experience where a smart individual insists on explaining everything that they know to you. Not only is it very boring at parties, it is also quite an inefficient form of communication. When asked a direct and simple question, these individuals can get stuck in the weeds explaining the process, knowledge, research and peer-reviewed opinions that stand behind the one sentence answer (which was all I was looking for).

What does this have to do with trust? Well, in their endeavor to overachieve on the credibility front, I don't know if I can trust them to think strategically and keep an eye on the bigger picture.

Conversely, I am a big picture thinker. I rely on a team of highly capable specialists and detailed thinkers. Because they have earned my trust over the years, I can use their opinions to do my strategic job. This makes it very difficult for other "detail-smart" people to trust me. In their eyes, I don't have the personal research and knowledge and peer-reviewed opinions to back up what I am personally saying and that hurts my credibility (in their eyes).

If I'm looking for broad, strategic credibility and they are looking for deep, narrow credibility *we will never trust each other.*

Obviously, this is unhelpful. It has been critical for me to be very aware of this and cater for this in my personal leadership operating model so that I can still gain the trust of these kinds of personality types and do my job as executive manager effectively.

YOUR AUTHENTIC LEADERSHIP STYLE AND STORY

Putting all this together, you will gain greater insight into understanding and developing your authentic leadership style. Time and again I have said to my managers:

> **IT IS NO USE EMULATING RICHARD BRANSON'S LEADERSHIP STYLE IF YOU ARE AN ELON MUSK.**

You may be successful for a couple of hours, but it will be inauthentic, and people will see through it. And, as we have seen from the trust equation, this will immediately diminish your credibility and reliability and damage trust.

Taking what you have learned from introspection, personality profiling and 360-degree feedback will enable you to better hone your natural leadership style and help you develop the strengths surrounding that style. I'm including here some leadership style descriptors that I have found useful when working with my teams, managers and executives[6]. The objective is introspection and is aligned to a set of descriptors that can guide our self-awareness and personal development.

Note: It is *not* important to isolate your leadership style to one descriptor. They aren't mutually exclusive and sometimes you can, very appropriately, have a different style with different staff. Pick one. Pick two. Or pick three.

Personally, I am a combination of an authoritative and advisory leader, depending on circumstance. And this fits perfectly with my strong self-preservation Enneagram 8 personality type.

---

[6] Taken from a collation by Hassan, Asad and Hoshino, Determinants of Leadership Style in Big Five Personality Dimensions; *Universal Journal of Management 4(4)*: 161-179, 2016 at https://www.hrpub.org/download/20160331/UJM2-12105627.pdf

Autocratic Leadership: Punitive, less concerned for socio-emotional dimension of group, dominating, dictatorial, unilateral decision making

Democratic Leadership: Considerate, participative, concerned with maintaining relationships with others, group decision making

Laissez-faire Leadership: Lack of involvement, avoidance of responsibilities, resistance in discussing critical issues

Transactional Leadership: Leader-follower exchanges, clarification of subordinate responsibilities, contingent rewards

Task-oriented Leadership: Planning and organizing work activities, clarification of roles, resolving work-related problems, focus on goal achievement

Interpersonal Leadership: Tactful, enthusiastic, encouraging, confidence builder, morale booster, motive arouser, honest, sincere, trustworthy, extrovert

Transformational Leadership: Vision, inspirational communication, intellectual stimulation, influence, empowerment, high performance expectations

Charismatic Leadership: Strategic vision, unconventional behavior, agents of change, sensitive to the needs of followers, risk orientation, extrovert

Distributed Leadership: Collaborative, intuitive working-relations, institutionalized practices

Participative Leadership: Shared decision making, values others' input, seek consensus, increased autonomy and empowerment to subordinates

Directive Leadership: Issuing instructions and commands, assigning goals, providing members with a framework for decision making

Ethical Leadership: Awareness for others, considerate, honest, altruistic, caring, principled, internal locus of control, proactive, co-operative

Authoritative Leadership: Assertive, supportive, demanding, responsive, manipulative, paternalistic

Authoritarian Leadership: Self-oriented, rigid, defensive, apathetic, assertive, abusive, exploitive, task-oriented, low responsiveness

Intellectual Leadership: Clear vision, higher level of cognitive ability, conscientious, proactive, free from fear, self-regulated, challenge status quo

Instrumental Leadership: Neurotic, require high commitment from followers, task and goal oriented, functionalist approach

Coercive Leadership: Conformity, repressed creativity, aggressive, inflexible, use of threat, self-centered, authoritarian, fear-driven

Team-oriented Leadership: Collaborative, team integrator, prefers status quo, encourage diversity, democratic, supportive, conflict manager

Delegative Leadership: Procedural fairness, low need for dominance, shared power, motivate subordinates, seek consensus, maintains relationships

Autonomous Leadership: Individualistic, encourage novelty, disrupts existing policies, facilitates knowledge transfer, responsible for task accomplishment

Coaching Leadership: Facilitator, authentic, compassionate, candid, interpersonally sensitive, develop people for future, motivating

Affiliative Leadership: Motivator in stressful time, creates harmony among team, empathetic, conflict reducer, low on consultation, relationship oriented, visionary

Supportive Leadership: Interpersonal trust, environment conducive to psychological well-being of followers, employee empowerment, provides support to followers, caring

Relationship-oriented Leadership: Concern and respect for followers, express appreciation and support, build friendly and supportive relationships

Consultative/Advisory Leadership: Provide professional guidance to followers, operate in less ambiguous situation, low external and high internal locus control

Humane-oriented Leadership: Fair, altruistic, compassionate, modest, strong labor representation, social welfare, benevolent, motivational, interpersonal relationship

Expressive Leadership: Anti-authoritarian, interpersonally sensitive, grant autonomy, relationship motivated leadership, socio-emotional

Visionary Leadership: Emotionally expressive, interpersonally sensitive, foresight, proactive, inspirational, guide and empower followers, change status quo

Pacesetting Leadership: Sets high standard and expects excellence from subordinates, authoritative, high on conscientiousness

Narcissist Leadership: Self-centered, status conscious, conflict inducer, unsympathetic, haughty, exploitive, seek attention, aggressive, unforgiving nature

E-leadership: Swift, more toward autonomy, flexible in dynamic environment, expertise in building and leading networks

Achievement-oriented Leadership: Maintain high level of performance, set challenging goals, strive for excellence, show confidence in followers, high internal locus of control

Authentic Leadership: Morally courageous, pro-social behavior, reliable, honest, social justice and equality, optimistic, self-disciplined, self-expressive

Servant Leadership: Steward, follower-centric, altruistic, commitment for growth of people, strong spiritual values and beliefs

Citizen Leadership: Egalitarian, commitment for growth of people, bring constructive change, democratic, inspirational, innovative, team-oriented

Aversive Leadership: Relies on coercive power, authoritarian, cynical, exploitive, engage in intimidation and dispensing reprimands, aggressive

Empowering Leadership: Concerned with employee performance and satisfaction, grant autonomy, share power, agreeable, team-oriented, encourage self-development

Opinion Leadership: Dominant, persistent, social; confident, high degree of social maturity innovativeness, withstand powerful social inhibitors

Self-protective Leadership: Status conscious, self-centered, conflict-inducing, procedural and face-saving

Your leadership story

Pulling all of this together, it is now useful for you to craft your leadership story. The introduction to this book contained pertinent parts of my leadership story—presented to provide credibility and context to who I am and my opinions on life. Life is a series of chapters, and each chapter has its own unique context, characters, crises and learnings. Pulling this together into a short but professionally colorful narrative is helpful.

I use different aspects of my leadership story when I interview new senior managers and executives, for example. It is important for them to get a good sense of who I am, why I am here and how I operate. We are potentially going to be working closely together. The richer and more accurate that story is, the more effective the corporate dating process.

Some of us are not very nostalgic. So, taking some time to re-live your professional and leadership journey may elicit some useful insights into why you do things the way you do. It will also remind you of past learning experiences and specific moments of insight. These collections of color are useful in self-reflection and are invaluable for coaching and inspiring those around us.

We will talk about the "dot-dash" tool later in **manage style**. Until we get there, consider writing the Contents Page for the story of your professional life. What are the main chapters? Who are the main characters that played key roles? What are the significant circumstances and situations?

Why do this? It will give you greater insight into who you are as a leader and help you relate more richly to your leadership qualities as you continue to move forward and master them. Also, it will help you answer this question: What is your next chapter?

What is your next chapter?

How can you lead, coach and develop your team members, and best prepare them for their next chapter in life, if you aren't clear on your next chapter?

- What do you want to master in your current role?
- What is available for you to master in your current role? What isn't?
- How long have you been in this role?
- What have you learned from your current leader? What more is there to learn?
- What can't they teach you?
- Where will you learn that? Now or in your next role?

It is very healthy to know where you are going. And it is pretty obvious that you won't be with your current employer/business for the next 20 years. Being proactive and transparent about your current chapter, what you are there to learn, and when it is time to move up or on, is a very mature professional approach. But, read the room before giving two-years' notice. Not all leaders are used to, or prepared for, working this way.

Knowing your story, where you would like it to go, and taking responsibility for getting there, is executive thinking.

YOUR LEADERSHIP HEATMAP

Structured heatmaps are very useful executive tools. The first one I would recommend is for understanding your personal "hot spots." Draw off the leadership style's introspection and any (thorough) personality profiling work that you have properly grappled with and build your leadership heatmap.

At the end of the previous chapter, I listed some of the key aspects of successful executive thinking across the 5S Model. Use these as your big buckets. Now, take your key characteristics—5 to 10 of them to be comprehensive—and for each of the 5S aspects, reflect on and write down (in a spreadsheet, OneNote, whatever):

- How could my characteristics *help* me in this aspect of executive thinking?
- How could my characteristics *hurt* me in this aspect of executive thinking?

Now, obviously, we have only just started on our 5S journey, but set it up, and as we run through the different areas, go back, and reflect on what green and red would look like for your personality and leadership style.

> **WHERE SOMETHING IS RED BECAUSE IT DEMANDS A CHARACTERISTIC THAT IS NOT INHERENT IN YOUR PERSONALITY MAKE UP—YOU NEED TO THINK ABOUT HOW TO STRUCTURALLY CATER FOR THAT!**

Back to principle numero uno: People don't change. So, if there is a part of you that isn't naturally pre-disposed toward some element of executive thinking, you need to figure out how you can create a structural support to help you cover that hotspot. If you're hoping to cover it by growing some new characteristic, then you're reading the wrong book.

An example: I have never been accused of being the life of the party. In social settings, I am pretty introverted. And I suck at small talk. Even worse, I loathe talking about sports that people support but don't play, regardless of what team they were on at high school. The problem is that being a positive energy contributor, being able to engage people socially—especially extroverts—is an important part of leadership. If I buried my head in the sand or avoided bigger work functions, I would be a very ineffective leader.

I do, however, love connecting with people one-on-one. I deliberately invest time in connecting with people in one-on-ones. I have regular coffees, brunches, lunches—in person or virtually—to connect with my management team members. I build a lot of emotional bank account that way. And I learn more about people's motivations and lives than their day-to-day work.

Example: A month before a year-end function, I was having a one-on-one with one of my managers. They mentioned that one of their star performers, Roxanne, was in a good space because they had just bought a new house.

I didn't immediately reach out and congratulate Roxanne. I sought her out at the year-end function, had a 30-minute conversation with her about the house, the process, and their ideas, as we flipped through the pictures on her phone. She was surprised I knew about it and was eager to share her excitement with me. It was great to connect with her on something meaningful that wasn't work related. It was so much more effective in person than through a one-liner email.

To help me perform better in larger social settings (which I'm not naturally good at), I leverage my extensive one-on-ones to build trust outside of these events and so have meaningful things to talk about at these events.

That's what I mean by a structural support.

In a sales environment, I am great at being a facilitative consultant, but, again, I'm not the life of the party. So, I am very conscious about the personalities I hire and surround myself with to make up for my lack of extroverted sales characteristics.

Back to our heatmap: I have often looked at dynamic extroverts in these situations with envy. But that's just not me. And pretending to be that will be both exhausting and inauthentic. So, I have found ways to constructively work with my fundamental leadership characteristics to cover that base.

IF YOU ARE NATURALLY...	HOW DO YOU...
Disorganized Spontaneous	Keep track of what's important with systems, reminders and more frequent personal ac-countability check-ins
A perfectionist	Test, learn and accept what can be "good enough" instead of perfect, so as to not discourage people unnecessarily
A conflict avoider Passive aggressive	Use tools and logic to stand up for yourself constructively. Proactively use your team
Introverted	Remember to bring authentic energy to all in-teractions and not seem disengaged
Decisive	Drive collaboration and engagement with the team to ensure they are shaping the answer and not left behind
Empathetic and connect with people easily	Gauge when you are letting emotional attachment cloud objective judgment
Detail oriented	Keep track of the bigger picture and remember to balance your communications (top-down vs bottom-up)

Here is an abridged example for two characteristics of my personality and leadership style.

Tom Gardner		
Enneagram	8	Self Preservation
Leadership Styles	Authoritative	Advisory

DECISIVE WITH HIGH ACTION ORIENTATION	
Strength	Doesn't get caught up in analysis paralysis. Maintains direction. Team clear on Tom's position.
Blindspot	Could leave team members behind who need more time to decide, or buy into a direction. May decide on incomplete analysis and miss something.
Support	Tom talks last in meetings where decisions are made—giving everyone else the opportunity to give and work through their views.
	Leverage Enneagram to consciously give slower decision makers time to decide and buy in. Design preparation time before meetings, and time between meetings and decisions to enable this.
	Get support of thinking-centered executives to balance analysis with action—use an explicit check-in agenda item in executive meetings.

DIRECT, COMFORTABLE WITH CONFLICT	
Strength	Team knows where they stand—no hidden agendas or "what is Tom thinking?" Radical candor as a development tool. Open and transparent on difficult topics. Puts the elephant on the table for more effec-tive problem solving.
Blindspot	Style could scare conflict avoiders. Passive-aggressive team members would not meet Tom halfway on difficult topics.
	Team members can use Tom to solve conflicts they should learn to deal with themselves.
Support	Over-invest in trust building, maintain emotional bank accounts—one-on-ones with all key stake-holders at least monthly. Leverage other leaders for backstage check-ins to identify any clean up requirements—put an item on the exec meeting agenda to "discuss key staff" and any actions required.

In a stand-alone document, I would cover at least five characteristics and flesh out the blocks into even more meaningful descriptions with specifics.

For example: Bob on the executive team is a passive-aggressive five so I would work with the CEO and the executive team to structure executive meetings accordingly. We would problem-solve how to effectively and efficiently structure meeting prep, one-on-ones and exec meeting processes to work through issues, while balancing perspectives and needs across the Enneagram eight-five polarities.

It takes thought, creativity and collaboration. And it starts with self-awareness and effort. This is a key foundation that we will keep building on through the other Ss.

Manage self is hard. And one of the hardest things about it is not climbing back up Mount Ignorance as we work on ourselves—either through false self-confidence or by slipping back into old habits and ignoring the lessons we have learned. Ego and our emotions make this an ongoing, material risk.

When your team and staff find the courage to give you the rich, honest feedback that you have asked for and you then don't do anything with it, that seriously impacts trust and inspirational leadership.

Work with your team, your colleagues, your leaders, coaches, your significant other and your friends to help keep you honest with yourself and on track. Your career as an executive manager will thank you.

MANAGE SELF TO-DO LIST

☐ Invest in a good and comprehensive personality profiling assessment—extra points if you have coaching sessions to really understand the framework and your assessment.

☐ Build a 360-degree feedback survey template. Run your 360-degree feedback survey annually.

☐ Write your leadership story. Capture the sections underpinning your leadership development that you can use when coaching your team members.

☐ Build your management heatmap and keep a working copy on your desktop.

☐ Work with your team to design mutually beneficial structural supports for your hotspots.

MANAGE STRATEGY

"Anticipate. Don't Improvise."

—THE KILLER, PLAYED BY MICHAEL FASSBENDER

T he fundamental purpose of a people leader is to keep people on track. One of the biggest secrets of great executive thinking is: Proactively keeping people on track is infinitely easier and more rewarding than reacting to things being off track.

In this section, we are going to briefly explore strategy, vision, mission and values and how you can think about these in the context of your function and department.

As a leader, having a guiding strategic light to move your team toward inspires the team with tangible purpose and ensures their efforts are aligned with ultimate company value.

We will capture this in a strategic narrative that will help you guide quarterly and annual strategic efforts.

Taking this a tactical step further into Objectives and Key Results (OKRs) is the key to moving the needle in a strategically focused way.

We will then take a walk through executive problem solving, thinking and reflections to help you stay the course and be a useful thought partner week to week.

Finally, we will briefly discuss managing up, and how to think about showing your boss all the good stuff you are up to, which is adding value in their lives.

THE STRATEGIC PROCESS

EXECUTIVES DON'T WAIT FOR SHIT TO HAPPEN. EXECUTIVES MAKE SHIT HAPPEN.

Knowing you are making the *right* shit happen is critical. And this starts with strategy at every level.

One of the biggest things holding intermediate managers back in this regard is having only a tactical or operational view of the business. Without a strategic mindset of your role, function or portfolio, it's hard to self-direct "what's next" beyond the immediate tactical plans.

One of my marketing leads was getting frustrated with their development and progress. I clearly remember their "Aha!" moment in this regard:

> Stacey was getting frustrated with a sense of stunted growth. As with all growth and development, she needed to figure out what mindset was holding her back. One of her issues was that she was waiting to be told what to do and what to focus on. This isn't a self-driven mindset. This is a "junior mindset." So, I asked her: "If we had a senior marketing manager join the business tomorrow, what would they do? How would they show up and start operating?"

That provided a lot of mental clarity for Stacey. She visualized a smart, experienced person arriving and asking strategic questions, having executive debates around it, putting together a brand and marketing **strategy** *and driving an annual marketing plan for the next year.*

Suddenly, Stacey was in the driver's seat. She put together a tight brand and marketing strategy document. She held several great working sessions with the execs and managers around this. And it ended in a solid marketing strategy and plan for the year ahead. It was great, and she was driving.

Stacey started with **thought leadership** *and aligned everyone around a* **strategy** *document and a plan. Most importantly, this new strategic perspective and framework could keep her in the driver's seat for years to come.*

Having a strategy document to mold problem solving helped Stacey push the thinking forward in a structured and progressive way. In six months or a years' time, she would have a familiar structure to rally everyone around and a good base of thinking to start from and revise—effective and efficient.

EXECUTIVE MANAGERS KNOW THAT PEOPLE ARE BAD AT READING MINDS. START WITH STRATEGY. A STRATEGY DOCUMENT!

Strategy remains widely misunderstood. Most professionals start getting a taste for strategy way too late in their careers. This exacerbates the problem. There is general group think that strategy only happens at the top. Company strategy is all there is.

This isn't true. Strategy and strategic thinking should happen at all levels of the organization. Most of the frustration I see in senior managers comes from their staff not focusing on priorities or stuff that will really move the needle. And a lot of this comes from them not being able to cascade a sense of strategic thinking.

The other side of the coin is that managers and staff are equally frustrated that they don't know what the priorities are. They, too, are frustrated by having to work in a strategic vacuum with no priorities or purpose.

Let's start by contextualizing strategy and where it fits into our daily lives.

1. We start with company strategy—this is developed with a three- to five-year view. Given we are investing in certain products, resources, technology, marketing campaigns, etc., we need a good longer-term idea of how we want to be positioned in the market to compete.

2. Next, we take that strategy and rally the troops around it. We create stories, a vision and missions to make the strategy real; we paint a picture of where we are going in the short and medium term.

3. We distill these further into strategic objectives and focused strategic projects. We set targets with KPIs.

4. We revise and adapt all the above at relevant intervals with the learnings we are gaining along the way.

5. KPIs and strategic projects let us know if we are successful in the short term.

We adapt and change our objectives and strategic projects in response to what we are learning.

These roll up into quarterly reviews of our missions.

Annually, we take broader stock to see if our overall strategy is still relevant. If we have learned something new, then we need to adapt our strategy or pivot.

Obviously, not everything we do is strategic. Paying salaries is a monthly base task in running a business—it needs to happen to keep the lights on. But everything we do—to serve a customer, not lose ground to a competitor, grow, improve, adapt, change culture, partner, work differently—should align with a strategic priority. As we will see in a bit, the above flow was written at a company level. You can and should be doing this at functional and departmental levels.

Time, attention and focus are finite resources

Energy and inspiration are correlated and you and I, and our staff, do not have endless time. So, we need to focus attention, energy and inspiration where it matters. We need to run the business and change the business. In between our business-as-usual tasks, personal lives, company politics, we have limited time for strategic projects and change. So, being clear on strategy and purpose has two key benefits:

- · It inspires. Knowing what I am doing will have impact, and influence company strategy; it will make me more engaged and focused. Inspired people are happier and more productive people. We all want that.

- · It makes the most use of scarce resources. We want to make sure that we are spending time on improvements, change, and projects that really matter. We want to strategically prioritize our teams' time, focus and attention.

THIS INCLUDES KNOWING WHAT TO SAY "NO" TO.

What is strategy?

"Developing interesting and useful strategy" is a whole other book. In the context of executive thinking, let's cover the essentials.

STRATEGY IS A DELIBERATE POSITION IN THE MARKET USED TO DELIVER A PRODUCT OR SERVICE TO A CUSTOMER IN LINE WITH A COMPETITIVE ADVANTAGE, ONE WHICH WILL SATISFY A NEED RELATIVE TO COMPETITION.

Strategy is a starting point with a deliberate vision. As we go forth and deliver and compete, we learn and adapt and pivot. Plans are how we want to build our business and go out and compete. Strategy is why we are doing it that way.

Know what your strategy is

Strategy isn't something that happens only in the boardroom or in Harvard Business Review case studies. Every function and department in a business fits into the business strategy—and has *its own* strategy that links to the business strategy. I seldom use "famous company" examples but this one is appropriate.

Consider Nike's strategy:

NIKE, INC. IS A GROWTH COMPANY.

We create innovative, must-have products. We build deep, personal connections with consumers. And we deliver an integrated marketplace with compelling retail experiences.

How does this apply to a department?

Same same. A department has customers. You can have a highly tech-leveraged strategy, a low-cost strategy, a high-complexity strategy, a bare-minimum strategy, an innovation-led strategy, a safe strategy, etc. etc.

Now, consider Nike's risk and compliance department. Do you think their mandate is to build deep, personal connections with consumers? To innovate and boldly go where no compliance officer has gone before?

Hell no.

But that department does have a strategy. It has to fit into and enable the broader innovation strategy of Nike. It also needs to not hinder that strategy while protecting the business and its customers.

The benefit that a functional and department leader has is that they can anchor their strategy in the broader business strategy. One of the best tools I have used for defining a functional and departmental strategy actually comes out of marketing and is called a brand positioning statement.

Brand positioning statement

The Brand positioning statement (BPS) helps you spell out who your customers are, what value you add to them, and how you are different or distinctive.

The framework looks like this:

*For (**customer**) who (**has a need or opportunity**)*
*(**The department**) is a (**department category**) that*
*(**statement of key benefit**)*
*Unlike (**competing alternative/other way of running**
such department)*
*(**The department**) (**statement of primary differentiation**).*

Product example: Nike

*For **any active human being**, who is **looking to improve their**
athletic performance and be the best self they can be
Nike is **at the forefront of sportswear and sports product**
design and innovation
Unlike **traditional, product-centric footwear and**
apparel manufacturers:
Nike strives to bring inspiration and innovation to every
athlete [7] **in the world***

Department example 1: A people department in an industrial company:

The people team are the custodians and drivers of the employee value proposition, manager value proposition and community value proposition, providing the necessary people skills, support and frameworks to inspire our team and make our staff proud.

Unlike traditional and transactional HR teams like the people police.

---

[7] If you have a body, you are an athlete.

The people team enables and empowers connection and cohesion within the company—to help make Company Y a workplace our people want to brag about.

Department example 2: For the department above, we identified the management team as a unique sub-audience that they served so:

For all Company Y leaders, who want a trusted people partner for:
- *Guidance and direction on all people topics*
- *Management skills, coaching and learning*
- *Problem solving and a sounding board*

The people team owns and delivers the management value proposition, empowering and enabling our leaders through proactive, trusted engagement and by providing forward thinking innovation on all things people—unlike traditional, transactional, arm's length HR teams.

The people team builds great leaders and walks side by side with them to deliver on our vision and our Employee Value Proposition.

The BPS is a useful and fun framework to use with your team, your manager, and other managers to isolate and articulate where you fit in, what you do and how you are expected to do it differently.

Vision, mission and values

A strategy is a position. It is how you are going to approach and compete in the game. It doesn't tell anyone which tournament you are going to enter, which games you are playing or what kinds of players you want to recruit.

Vision: Which tournament are we setting out to win?

What do you want to be when you grow up? What is the big picture outcome? To be a world class risk and compliance department at the forefront of thinking in your industry? To be the best business-enabling risk and compliance department that everyone in the business loves working with?

Drawing from the BPS, how can you articulate the way in which your department should be positioned and feel in five years' time?

Mission: Which game are we playing next?

What is the short term, tangible goal that will drive us toward our vision? If we are successful at our missions, we will achieve our vision.

Values: What team culture are we building?

How do we want to play the game? What are the principles and standards of behavior with which we want to tackle our missions? Who are the kinds of people we want to work with on this journey, will make it a success and make it worthwhile day-to-day?

Simple example to demonstrate:

Vision: To be one of the world's greatest female mountaineers
Mission: To scale two of the Seven Summits in 2024
Values: To do it with female-only teams

It's important to highlight the link between vision and mission. Vision is what we want to be. If we are successful in our missions, what we achieve along the way, then we know we are fulfilling our vision destiny.

Mission = win the battle. Vision = ultimately winning the war (by winning enough key battles).

I joined my first startup a couple of years into my career. One of the biggest challenges I faced was the lack of a vision and mission. The vision/strategy/mission of the company at the time I joined was "to grow as fast as possible" and/or "to take advantage of opportunities."

You can't build a company culture around that. It isn't compelling for anyone but the founders/shareholders, it doesn't elicit purpose and meaning, and it certainly doesn't help prioritization of resources and efforts. In fact, it undermines that.

I went through a strategy development process with the board, execs, and management team and we defined our vision and mission:

Strategy/BPS: *For people living with HIV or diabetes, AllLife is a profit-with-purpose direct life insurance company. AllLife walks the journey with you—ensuring you do the right thing with your treatment, live a long, healthy life, and enjoy the benefits of competitive life insurance; unlike other life insurance providers who only talk to you when they have a fee increase.*

AllLife is for living.

Vision: *To be a distinctive profit-with-purpose life insurance provider for people with impaired lives*

Mission: *To be actively covering 60,000 clients by 2016.*

We chose that mission because there was a well-known stadium down the road that seated 60,000 people. We used the visual of imagining that stadium filled with all our clients, happy and celebrating.

In other businesses, we have used personas, and what we want our customers to say about us, to work alongside measurable targets.

> **BEING THOUGHTFUL AND CAPTURING THIS FOR YOUR FUNCTION OR DEPARTMENT PROVIDES A COMPELLING GUIDING LIGHT FOR HOW THEY FIT INTO THE BIGGER PICTURE.**

And that cascade is important. Think of it as a giant pyramid with the company vision, mission and values as the capstone. Each business unit's vision, mission and values sit under and support the company vision, mission and values. In turn, the functions and departments sit under and support that, so we all have an orchestrated and deliberate purpose in the greater scheme of things.

CASCADING STRATEGIC DIRECTION

Once you have contextualized your department/functional strategy, contextualizing and communicating this in a strategic narrative is a powerful inspirational leadership tool.

This showed up beautifully just the other day: We were doing some

360-degree feedback for the head of a global business unit I was working with (**manage self**). I asked one of their managers, *What could Natalie work on? The response: She has such good ideas—a good strategy—I just wish she would write it down!*

> **IF YOU WANT EVERYONE TO BE ON THE SAME PAGE, MAYBE YOU SHOULD START WITH A PAGE.**

A strategic narrative is just that. It is a one-page executive summary of where you are, where you are going and what is important. One pager doesn't get discussed and then filed. This is a *narrative* and it should be used, revisited and revised often. It is a working one pager.

> **REMEMBER: REPETITION IS A MANAGEMENT TOOL.**

People get caught up in the day-to-day. The further toward the frontline we travel, the more our team members are dodging bullets and digging trenches. It's easy for them to forget what war they are battling when they are mentally so far from home. Your strategic narrative ties this together. It provides the "why" and the "what." It gives a succinct narrative of where we are and what we are doing next.

Executive storytelling

Storytelling has become a bit of a fad in executive circles of late. This has led to a common misconception that good executive storytelling is like a Hollywood script or a riveting Dan Brown novel. While I do appreciate why and where storytelling can be useful, the gap between basic (poor) communication in business and hard-core Nike Jordan movie scripts is just too wide.

Executive storytelling is inspiring because it covers what is required to drive ***context, clarity and priority***. I find many people want to run before they can walk in the realms of professional storytelling.

Let's start with a basic example:

If you think about your favorite film. Not as a drawn-out, never-ending series; and not an 8-part Harry Potter opus but rather as a single 90-minute to 2-hour film. The script normally goes something like this:

> **We meet the characters, understand their lifestyles and their environment:** *Jim is 25, chronically single but is fundamentally a nice guy. Jill just started in accounting, is beautiful and has recently broken up with her long-term boyfriend. After some awkward scenes, Jim and Jill end up out on a date and all is good in the world.*

> **We meet the tragedy:** *Just as you are filled with hope for mankind, Jill receives a text from her ex, Josh. His father has passed away and he is having a mental health episode. Jill feels bad, invites Josh over to talk. One thing leads to another, Josh snogs Jill. Jim walks in. Catastrophe.*

> **We want to know how it ends:** *Despite Josh's father passing away, he remains an arsehole. Jill sees the error in her ways and feels terrible. Jim is boarding a plane to escape the deep despair of his life and work environment after the Jill embarrassment. As the airplane doors are closing, we see Jill run up to and pound on the aircraft door through the little window—and all is right in the world again.*

This is how every single film my wife chooses to watch goes. Every. Single. One.

Why? Because that narrative structure works. And this is it:

SITUATION > COMPLICATION > RESOLUTION (SCR)

Have a think through your favorite movie or novel and see if you can package it into an SCR.

The situation, complication, resolution (SCR) model

We will unpack engaging communication more holistically under our fifth S—**Manage Style**—in due course. For developing a compelling strategic narrative, we will explore the SCR Model. You can use this framework in almost every type of communication, even if changing dinner plans for Friday. I often start a meeting with the SC (situation/ complication) of the SCR. The point of the meeting is to determine the R (resolution).

Any good strategic communication covers these three elements:

- **Situation:** What is the pertinent context? What have we been focusing on? How did we hope the world would evolve? Why are we here?

- **Complication:** What have we learned? What has changed? What progress have we made? What issues have popped up?

- **Resolution:** What's next? What is the new path? What are the new priorities?

The value of the SCR is that it lays out the full story of what is happening so everyone is on the same page and has shared context.

Let's look at a couple of examples:

I recently sent an email to a branding consultant on a business I am helping set up. That's all the context I'm going to give you. Read the email:

Example 1: Email to branding consultant

Hi Kristin

I am looking for some help with the branding of a new company. Kate gave me your details and raved about your work.

Mary has just finished her immigration law qualification and will be open-ing her own emigration agency next year. Current agents are swamped and generally struggle to handle volume and scale their business. This results in poor customer service levels and anxious clients. FYI—I have a lot of experience in building businesses and brands. Mary has a lot of experience in law.

We are struggling to trade off brand identity and land on a name. The two angles are:

- *a more professional services brand like a law firm or accounting firm (you are dealing with a professional expert here)—where the main person is key. Even though there is a key person around which to build credibility, this can hamper scalability when you want clients to deal with other people in the business as a key point of contact.*
- *a more general professional services business identity and name.*

We have shortlisted a bunch of names and run a survey with friends and contacts who are immigrating as we speak. See attached results and commentary.

*We could use your expertise to **due diligence the names**, see if you come up with anything interesting/exciting that we haven't thought of; to **build a brand identity and feel** that balances professional services with approachability and aligns with the destination country; and **design the logo**, colors, iconography and fonts and package in a **brand guide**.*

Please let me know if you have any immediate questions or let us know when you are available to meet and workshop.

You can clearly see the situation > complication > resolution thread in the email content. As you can appreciate, this gave the consultant a real running start and eliminated a ton of inefficiency. She did admit at the end of the project that I was the most structured and organized person she had ever worked with. I appreciated that. Time is money.

Example 2: Go-To-Market SCR:

Our strategic focus for 2023 has been taking our new generative AI product to market. Focus has been on the banking sectors in Germany, the US, the

UK and Canada. The first half of the year saw great interest from existing clients, sales partners and high priority prospects.

As the sales cycles have evolved, it has become clear that we need integrations into third party software solutions that are different from the standard integration of our core product. Building these will require different expertise and resources and may introduce IP risk.

We are setting up a cross-functional task team to build a business case on whether this is feasible and advisable. This will be completed by the end of October to inform our AI strategy for 2024 and give us time to engage partners and clients on the outcomes.

This seems simple and obvious. Reading a good SCR often feels that way. But three cautionary points:

People are generally terrible at this. They assume everyone is on the same page in terms of context, so they "jump right in." They figure out everyone is on a different page much later—wasting valuable time and credibility.

IF THERE IS NO PAGE, HOW CAN EVERYONE BE ON THE SAME PAGE?

People don't repeat the narrative enough. *Surely, they all understand what we are doing from the exec presentation in January.* People have personal lives, day-to-day responsibilities, myriad collaboration points, staff to deal with and projects (theirs and others). Don't assume what pertains to your strategic narrative is top of mind to them.

REPETITION IS A KEY MANAGEMENT TOOL.

People compile and deliver strategic narratives so poorly that it sounds like they don't know what is going on. The professional SCR is *not* a movie script. It is a holistic but succinct narrative of why we are here and what we are going to do.

> TIGHT, SUCCINCT LANGUAGE AND IMPACTFUL WORD CHOICE IS CRITICAL.

So, back to strategic narratives. Using the SCR framework to have a succinct one pager of what is happening in the business and how it influences the next steps in your team/department/function is very empowering for your staff.

The strategic narrative will help you **ensure you are aligned with your senior leaders.** Getting them clear on your strategic narrative ensures they know where you're headed and why. Clearly and powerfully. They can spot gaps or redirect more efficiently. You can easily update it and circulate as things evolve.

The strategic narrative will help you **identify any change in driving force, uncertainty, lesson or other significant and relevant complication that you haven't accounted for** and that may impact the resolution. Using your narrative, your senior managers, your peers and your team can easily spot if something is missing from the cohesive thinking and help build more effective next steps.

The strategic narrative will help you **inspire your team. Understanding WHY they are doing what they are doing is purposeful.** Linking what they are doing to business or functional strategy gives them insight into the strategic thinking of the business—this is always inspiring.

Being a clear communicator of strategic narratives makes you an inspirational thought leader in the business. It will help you achieve better outcomes, influence more effectively and be someone others take joy in working with *because they don't need to read your mind to know what the hell is going on.*

If you were to analyze the most impactful emails you have sent or received, or even the most impactful text messages, chances are they follow the situation—complication—resolution thread. Aligning on why we are here, being clear on what the real challenge is, and then proposing a clear path forward that addresses the challenge in light of the situational context; that is powerful executive storytelling.

Scenario planning

Working with managers, from team leaders all the way up to executives, I have found linear thinking to be one of the biggest things that hold people back in high-performance environments. Here I want to unpack some practical concepts and ideas around scenario planning. Thinking, questions and ideas you can take with you to have more impact in your role on Monday.

I want to use a quick analogy that you can take with you—to guide you and to help you empower your team and your peers to better understand scenario planning. Let's assume you have a break coming up and you are thinking about a road trip from New York to San Francisco.

1. You hop onto Google Maps and find the best route.

2. You are going to allocate two weeks to the trip so you can take in the sites and culture. You'll need to stay in hotels or Airbnbs along the way.

3. You break the 3,000 miles (4,700 km) into reasonable and interesting chunks, and you book your accommodation.

4. You hit up Trip Adviser, find some well-rated sites and restaurants and put an itinerary together.

5. You pack the car. You leave. You have a blast.

   This is a plan. This demonstrates planning.

Now, let's rewind 400–500 years.

You want to travel from New York (or whatever it was called) to San Francisco (ditto) in the 1500s.

1. You pack your bags.

2. You hop on your horse.

3. You load your six-shooter.

4. You say a prayer.

5. You leave.

In our 1500s example, we need scenario planning. We have a bunch of questions that we need to ask ourselves about our trip and we need to think through the possible answers to those questions. We then need a variety of plans (plural) to cater to those answers and potential eventualities.

We know where we want to end up. We know our starting direction. We have healthy horses, a non-perishable food supply and water. We have a plan for the first couple of days. But we do not know what is over that yonder hill. We don't know how long the journey is going to take. We need a strategy for subsistence. We need a strategy for collecting and carrying water. And we need a strategy for protection from creatures and the elements:

If we find clean water, then we will collect it. If we don't find clean water, then we will dig for it.

We are good hunters. If we find wild animals, then we will hunt them. If we don't find wild animals, then we will forage. We will have to bring along a foraging expert.

If we find expanses of barren land, then we will have to re-route south and lengthen the journey as we know it is more temperate there. We will trade off distance and time for food and water.

If we cannot find a way and are in dire straits, we will stop in Chicago or Denver. If we re-route that far south and cannot make it to the Rockies, we will head to Houston.

You can now appreciate how drastically different a plan and a strategy are in these two examples.

Strategy can be thought of as:

1. We have a good idea of where we want to go/end up.

2. We know what is important for that outcome.

3. We know what our strengths and capabilities are.

4. We have some initial choices to make and some things we will learn along the way.

5. There is a lot we don't know. We do not have a crystal ball. Hope is not a management tool. So, we have thought through some scenarios and *how we will change our plan to cater to those possibilities.*

This would yield good strategy and scenario planning for getting from New York to San Francisco in the 1500s.

Where does strategy and scenario planning work together?

As we have seen, strategy applies everywhere.

CORPORATE STRATEGY >BUSINESS STRATEGY > FUNCTIONAL STRATEGY > DEPARTMENT STRATEGY > ANNUAL > MONTHLY > WEEKLY

When a great manager approaches a one-on-one with a member of their team, they have choices to make. Complex choices about what to cover and how to cover it. To be inspiring? To be harsh? To take a micro view of the past week? To have a chat about personal three-year plans and career progression?

All these choices need to be contextualized to determine the best plan to approach this with. But if we are met with feedback/energy/thinking that means it is in our best interests to explore a different avenue or approach, then we are prepared for that. That may mean a different route, different skills, different business model, or even a different destination for the organization.

Good strategists appreciate the famous quote by General Dwight D. Eisenhower: *"Planning is essential. But plans are useless."*

So, how does scenario planning practically work?

Strategy and scenario planning go hand-in-hand as there is so much we don't know. To integrate the two, we follow a five-step process:

DEFINE STRATEGY > IDENTIFY DRIVING FORCES > DETERMINE UNCERTAINTIES > DEVELOP SCENARIOS > SET A STRATEGIC INTENTION

Define strategy:

- What are we here to achieve?
- What do we need (resources)?
- What are we good at?
- What competencies do we need to build?

Identify driving forces:

- What is the big picture context that is influencing us?
- What are the key sets of broader choices that we have to approach this?
- How are others playing the game? Why have they chosen this approach?

Determine uncertainties of the key driving forces:

- What do we know for sure?
- What have we mastered?
- What are we unsure about?
- What do we have to learn?
- What are the most important?

Develop scenarios:

- How could the future play out?
- We could learn x, or we could learn y; We could get good at x or we may fail to develop that competence.
- Paint the pictures. What would the world look like under each condition?

Set a strategic intention:

- What are our short-term If... then...? If we learn x, what does that mean? Hence, if we learn y, what does that mean?
- What do we do under these conditions?
- What are the implications for the team/department/business? How does this change the resources that we need? Where do we invest time, money and attention?
- How does it change what we need to be good at to still win?

How does this apply to Monday?

I am pretty sure when you walked through the steps above, you thought about examples of business- or company-wide strategy.

Now, go back through the steps and think about one of your key team members and what they need to get done this year.

- What are their strategic objectives for the year that tie into where you need to move the department and function and business?
- How have you aligned on tackling those objectives? What are you going to try? What do you need to learn? What could stand in the way? What stretch targets have you set yourselves?
- What are you going to check in on monthly and quarterly to know if you are on the right track? If you aren't, have you thought through the other tracks you will take?

If you have really thought this through as a manager, you can see how easy it is now to set meaningful overall objectives for the month, quarter, year. You can have an effective quarterly strategic review with this team member. You can more easily decide what kind of engagement you need to have with that team member this month:

- Has a driving force structurally changed?
- This is what we learned last month and how we need to change our attack.
- This is what we need to double down on this month.
- This is what we need to try, and to learn, next month.

You can directly answer, for the week:

- How are they doing with what they need to focus on and achieve?
- What's getting in the way of what they are trying to figure out/learn?
- Do they need inspiration and help to keep going? Do they need thought leadership? Resources?
- Do they need to change plans?

A tactical example:

> **A team member seems disengaged. They are quieter than usual and appear distracted in meetings and one-on-ones. Another team member has also noted this.**

A great manager will think through:

Objective: What is this team member's current big picture objective? Professionally and personally. Where do they fit into my big picture objective? They are one of my top performers.

Driving forces: What has been structurally getting in the way? What have they been trying to tackle? What came up in our last personal check-in? What do I know has changed in the bigger picture? We just announced a company-wide cost cutting.

Uncertainties: What uncertainties can I remove: What else could it be? One of their parents has been ill but they said the parent had turned the corner and was getting better. Has that changed?

Scenarios: What are the different ways I could engage this team member? Do I do it? Do I get one of their close team members to initially check in and remove some uncertainties before I engage? Should I have a social check-in, either virtual or in person, over coffee/drink/lunch?

Intent: If they bring up x, what is my response and plan? If it's y, what do I do?

Great executives go through this mental process minute by minute on the fly.

> APPRECIATING THAT THERE ARE DIFFERENT ANGLES TO THINGS, AND WORKING THROUGH THE DIFFERENT SCENARIOS THAT CAN PLAY OUT, IS KEY TO ANTICIPATING AND NOT IMPROVISING.

Working "in parallel"

In reality, we don't move forward on one path and wait for something to happen to change to a different track. Often, we run parallel streams of thinking and doing until we have learned more and need to commit to one overarching approach.

Early in the journey of one of my startups, we were moving from product market-testing specific product ideas and features with particular clients, to fully scalable product development. We had to move from a very target-product approach to a scalable, more generalist approach. As we moved into the next phase of growth, we were bulking up the team and bringing on new managers to take on more portfolios.

This is obviously a time of change and anxiety. Moving a team from a known way of working to a new, unknown way of working, is stressful. The management team was looking for clarity on the way forward. They were looking for a plan.

The problem was that the plan was heavily dependent on what people we could find. If we could find an executive who was an industry expert and fit the culture, they would lead the charge on the change in operating model. However, if we found a good generalist leader to add to the team, we would need to find subject matter experts to hire under them to support them, or find a good consultant.

I kept getting questions like: "Okay, so you agree we are hiring a consultant?"

The answer was obviously no. What we were doing was four things in parallel:

1. *Looking for consultants for whom we could get good referrals from our network.*
2. *Continuing to hire for the executive role and seeing what profiles came up.*
3. *Looking for suitable subject matter experts.*

4. *Learning new stuff about changes needed every day.*

Once we had started making inroads into these four workstreams, we would learn stuff. In learning stuff, we would tackle uncertainties and determine the trade-offs we were left with. The right structural strategy would emerge and then we could align on a forward plan.

Strategic planning with Gantt charts, or, at least, thinking in Gantt charts, can really help drive parallel working efficiency.

When is scenario planning inappropriate?

Scenario planning is vital when you have meaningful options, with significantly different outcomes, and you will only find out what the best route is over time.

Otherwise, it's just problem solving to find a solution. You may also consider scenarios that aren't time bound. *If we go with Salesforce, this is what the world will look like. If we go for Zoho, this is what the world will look like*—that's problem solving.

When having a clear plan is clouded by uncertainty that will become clearer over time, scenario planning is the answer.

In our search for certainty, we often inadvertently close doors to opportunity. Or we slow progress by tackling learnings one at a time. Thinking in scenarios and planning accordingly will make progress faster and de-risk the future.

Using questions and statements like:

· What are the scenarios?

· What are the different ways this could play out?

· Please put the scenarios on a page for us to discuss.

can help you drive more rigorous thinking and scenario planning in your function and departments.

We will deep-dive into collaboration in **manage synergy** but I'm sure you can appreciate how interesting and inspirational developing all of this with your team, your boss and your co-managers could be.

DRIVING FOCUS WITH OBJECTIVES AND KEY RESULTS (OKRS)

Once we have our strategy, vision and mission and we have considered scenarios to come up with a deliberate strategic plan, we need to get tactical.

OKRs have been around for over 50 years, but I still find many managers and executives who have never heard of them. If you have used OKRs, feel free to skip this section. There is great, comprehensive content and examples out there so, again, here are the essentials[8].

OKRs drive focus. I have been in numerous work environments where staff are snowed under and running from one focus area to the next and being very inefficient. In most cases, there isn't even a clearly defined strategy—but you have to appreciate that a strategy and mission are broader guideposts. They don't directly link to what I am doing right now. OKRs close that gap in a prioritized way.

In a nutshell, OKRS are:

Strategic **objective** 1: Clearly defined goal

- SMART **Key Result** 1
- SMART **Key Result** 2
- SMART **Key Result** 3

Sounds easy right?

It isn't. And the top-down approach I like to take is thinking through, with each manager:

Given our strategic narrative and priority themes for the year, what are the three to five objectives for the year that will move the needle in your sphere of influence?

OR

If you could only do three things this year to make a big difference in our performance and how we work, what would those three needle-moving things be?

---

8 https://www.whatmatters.com

I push for three to drive focus and then we end up with four or five.

We then break down the shorter-term scenario planning and plans and distill those into key results that are SMART:

- **S**pecific
- **M**easurable
- **A**ction oriented
- **R**elevant and realistic
- **T**imebound

Example: Let's consider the OKRs for one of the managers in a global business services (GBS) organization with the following strategic themes:

- *The GBS strategy for 2024 strives to "master basic operational excellence to deliver high quality, consistently and cost-effectively."*
- *Building on 2023 initiatives and learnings, 2024 will be a year of focus—aligned around core SLA delivery and stability. Focus on three strategic themes, complemented by functional and continental themes, will achieve this:*
- *Deliver quality through streamlined operations: Process mastery and transparency with our customers, to clear bottlenecks and grow.*
- *Deliver consistently through inspired, capable teams: Empowered and purposeful teams focusing on clear, priority outcomes.*
- *Capture cost advantages through agile technology adoption: Mastering agility and our technology to make delivery consistent and easier.*
- *Together, this will progress our vision to be a world class shared business service—delivering consistent high quality for our customers at a distinctive cost advantage.*

OKRs for one of the managers of accounts payable could look something like this:

- *Improve SLA delivery for accounts payable from 80% on time to 90% on time by end of FY*

- *Determine top 5 priority process bottlenecks by end Q1 (end-to-end business process mapping project)—business cases and project plans signed off*
- *Formally launch top 3 priority projects with customers beginning Q2 for intensive delivery by end Q3*
- *Launch next 2 priority projects beginning Q3 for intensive delivery by end Q4*
- *Q4 SLA audit to show >90% adherence, productivity and unit cost benchmarking to show 75P or above*

Ensure AP tech is fit for purpose—user and customer adoption at >95%

- *Issue logs and enhancement requests prioritized into change interventions with detailed project plans by end Q1*
- *Focused, agile system enhancements with IT concluded by end Q3*
- *New LMS chosen and implemented by end Q2*
- *User and customer adoption training and interventions concluded by end Q3*
- *Stability and adoption testing concluded by end Q4 to yield >95% adoption*

Improve culture and employee engagement to >80% for the business

- *Baseline employee engagement survey Q1*
- *Define culture strategy and assign culture teams Q1*
- *Conclude priority culture initiatives by end Q3 and re-run semi-annual employee engagement survey*

For each of these bullet points, I want to identify how I will know that something has been achieved or not.

- Have the culture teams been set up? Who is on what team? How many are there? What are their focus themes?

Then I know whether that key result has been achieved on time.

The best visual I have seen on OKRs is a road winding through hills. The objective is where you want to end up—the medium-term goal. The key results are the steps and milestones that get you to that goal. Setting out OKRs is prioritized strategic planning.

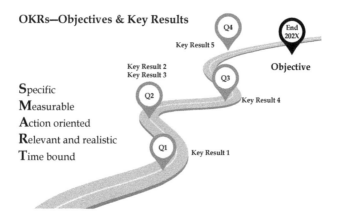

OKRs are traditionally measured on a scale of 100. I've seen different measurement scales, but the principles remain:

Red 0–30: we failed to make any significant progress.

Amber 40-60: we made progress but fell short of satisfactory impact.

Green 70–100: we achieved impact.

> **HOWEVER, IF YOU GET CAUGHT UP IN MEASURING OKRS THEN YOU MAY BE MISSING THE POINT.**

OKRs are a management tool. They are a way to communicate and align strategic priorities in a structured way. You should be checking in on KR progress monthly. You should have a strategic review and reflection on strategy and all OKRs quarterly. We want to be celebrating successes and proactively addressing any roadblocks so we can make headway toward our strategic destination.

A big part of these conversations is what is not a priority. There are a lot of things we could do this year and quarter. We can put those on a wish list and only structurally consider them once we know our OKRs are on track, and we have capacity.

> **REMEMBER: TIME, FOCUS AND ATTENTION ARE FINITE RESOURCES.**

If a new major idea or project pops up, which OKR does it put at risk? Or which OKR are you taking off the list?

Because OKRs are short and succinct—maximum one page or a single slide—they should be easy to remember, can be pulled up in monthly meetings and can be put up at your desk.

Quick check-in:

- We have our company, functional and department **strategy**.
- We have thought through our **vision, mission and values**.
- We have captured this in a compelling **strategic. narrative** to communicate this to all our teams, so they know what's going on and what's important.
- We have developed **OKRs** for everyone so we are clear on how we are going to move the needle this year and we will check in on these monthly (KRs) and quarterly (OKRs).

Now we need to problem solve.

EXECUTIVE PROBLEM SOLVING

Day-to-day problem solving—like figuring out why a system has gone down—is not executive problem solving. Executive problem solving involves many moving parts, trade-offs, collaboration and scenarios. Examples of executive problem solving would be:

- Developing a sales strategy
- Defining a product roadmap
- Revising a remote work policy
- Designing pricing tiers for a new product

Let me start with an example of where I see executive problem solving going wrong all the time.

I was a strategic adviser for an executive team. Like a lot of my consulting work, I was very hands on to make sure I knew what was really happening at different levels in the org and could give better, impactful strategic input. I was invited to an executive meeting and was sent an agenda. The third point on the agenda read: Sales Strategy Presentation. I knew immediately it was going to be a nightmare.

Max was the sales manager. He was an intermediate manager and had a lot to learn. I knew how this was going to play out. Max would have put a ton of work into this sales strategy presentation. Max wanted to impress the executives and shine.

From the first slide, it was clear that:

a) Max had put A LOT of time into this.

b) Max was missing some seriously important aspects of a sales strategy and hadn't included some important considerations of the business strategy.

c) Max had worked on this alone.

Now, this is a cluster[9] for three associated reasons:

a) Max had not only wasted a lot of time, but Max was also now extremely emotionally attached to this presentation. It was a "presentation" and not a draft. This was not a working session. It was now in a position where he wanted appreciation and recognition. A "good job."

b) Lack of a structured process meant that he hadn't uncovered obvious blind spots in thinking. Had he followed a structured strategic problem-solving process, he could have uncovered them himself. Had he even Googled "sales strategy" and looked at a couple of contents pages, he would have had a better executive view.

c) Lack of collaboration, especially with more strategic thinkers, meant that his answer was shit and his time and effort poorly spent, AND he couldn't use any of the team as co-sponsors and proponents of his strategy.

---

9 Abbreviated slang for a disastrously mishandled situation or undertaking.

Overall, this puts EVERYONE else in a very difficult position. Do we accept a crap strategy, so we don't hurt Max's feelings? How do we give feedback while tip-toeing through his pride? Where am I going to find time to deal with this unnecessary emotional fallout due to a poor problem-solving strategy.

Don't let this happen to you. Don't let this happen to your team members. Use an explicit and collaborative problem-solving strategy to manage time, attention and inspiration.

There are three models that I have used to good effect through my career:

- The **McKinsey seven-step problem-solving process** for strategic problem solving.
- The **design thinking process** for discrete problems.
- The **Five Whys framework** to push orders of thinking to identify root causes.

Structured problem solving

I have run numerous lectures, trainings and workshops on problem solving over the years. I start each one with a simple question:

Have you ever received training in problem solving?

The blank stares are exactly what I am looking for. Humans have been problem solving since before we stood upright. Millions of years later, we have think tanks, and offsites, and incubators, and and and—yet we still don't train ourselves, or our children, adequately in problem solving.

Similar to a personality profiling framework, having a couple of universal problem-solving approaches in your team will help you improve the quality of your problem solving, give you a common language to engage with on the problem-solving process and vastly improve collaborative efforts.

Overall philosophy: diverge then converge

An overall philosophy to problem solving is not fixating on finding a solution at the outset. I have tested this natural human inclination on numerous occasions with both professionals and business-school students. The first exercise I run in my problem-solving training sessions is to divide the group into small teams and ask them to solve: "Why did [country X] *not* win the world cup?"

They proceed to brainstorm the hell out of it. Randomly generating solutions and mind-mapping away, each one of them trying to immediately answer: *Because of y.*

We jump to conclusions. And our traditional schooling system encourages that. I ask a question. You give me the answer. Pass.

> WE AREN'T TAUGHT TO EXPLORE A PROBLEM OR ASK GOOD
> CLARIFYING QUESTIONS.

Life isn't like that. Problems are complicated. Strategic problems have contexts and perspectives and angles to them. Scenarios. Forces. We need to take the time to adequately **diverge** and explore and learn. Then we need to **converge** and narrow down to find some solutions.

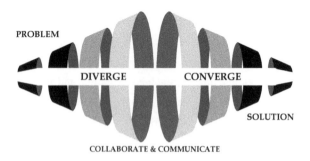

McKinsey's seven-step problem-solving process [10]

Tried and tested, McKinsey's seven steps are a great structured process to tackle even the most complex strategic problems. While the full seven steps will yield you the greatest results, key insights from each of the discrete steps will help you in any problem-solving process. Here are the steps in a nutshell with a McKinsey published diagram. Then we will run through each with my reflections, tips and tricks.

1. Define the problem
2. Structure the problem
3. Prioritize the focus areas
4. Work planning
5. Analysis
6. Synthesis
7. Recommendations and actions

Inherent to McKinsey's seven steps is the concept of diverge and then converge. We spend significant time in problem definition and structuring exploring the problem, the different aspects of the problem and how others have approached and solved the problem.

We then apply our minds and prioritize where we believe the most value lies. And then we go solve stuff.

Define the problem

Ensuring everyone is on the same page regarding why you are trying to develop a strategy or solve a problem really lays a solid foundation for the whole process. Giving the broader team a common ground of context and what has been tried before, what the key success factors are, and what success will look and feel like, is obviously valuable.

---

[10] https://www.mckinsey.com/capabilities/strategy-and-corporate-finance/our-insights/how-to-master-the-seven-step-problem-solving-process

This doesn't often happen. We launch into solution mode.

Having a project kickoff with all relevant project stakeholders centered around a problem statement worksheet is best practice.

Use a whiteboard, Miro, whatever, but take the time to explore what you are setting out to achieve and why, and get on the same page.

A problem statement worksheet typically includes rich discussions around six elements:

- A SMART problem statement
- **Strategic context:** situation and complication surrounding the problem or opportunity
- **Scope of solution:** where we should and should not play
- **Criteria for success:** when do we open the champagne? What are the hard and soft measurables that we have achieved success?
- **Key stakeholders:** decision makers, sources of insight, working team members and responsibilities, other people that may be impacted by the work and need to be consulted or informed
- **Barriers to impact:** what could impact the solutions or stand in our way that we need to take into account in the process and solution

As you can tell from many of these aspects, there is a lot we won't know up front. But, getting a collective download of what we do know, getting on the same page, and putting explicit pins in things we need to learn and come back to, gives the team an aligned running start.

THE DISCUSSION IS MORE IMPORTANT THAN THE END PRODUCT.

Capture and record insights in the problem statement worksheet but don't get caught up in gross accuracy and capturing everything. Rich discussions and an aligned view are the objective, not a perfect piece of paper.

Structure the problem

Structuring a problem is probably the hardest and most valuable step in the process. It's also the hardest to explain. Let's quickly explore what it isn't:

- Brainstorming
- Mind mapping
- Case studies
- Frameworks (are only an input into structuring)

The problem with all the above is that you have no built-in mechanism to test whether you have covered everything. Mind mapping stops when you get bored. You don't know if there is a big gap in the map. Just like Max didn't know there were big gaps in his sales strategy.

Structuring a strategic problem is an art. McKinsey uses issue trees to do this. Issue trees are "structured mind maps" in that they structure out thinking into buckets and branches that strive to be mutually exclusive and collectively exhaustive (MECE). This ensures that as much of the problem is explored as is possible. On the next page is an example of an issue tree for a go-to-market strategy that I built with a business development team to take a new product to market.

This is an actual issue tree I used. There are overlaps and things missing—sure. However, I want you to take note of one important thing:

ISSUE TREES ALLOW YOU TO READ MY MIND! THEY GIVE COMPLETE CLARITY—WITHIN TWO MINUTES—OF HOW I AM THINKING ABOUT THE PROBLEM.

Can you appreciate how this both improves the rigor of problem solving *and* drastically improves and accelerates collaboration?

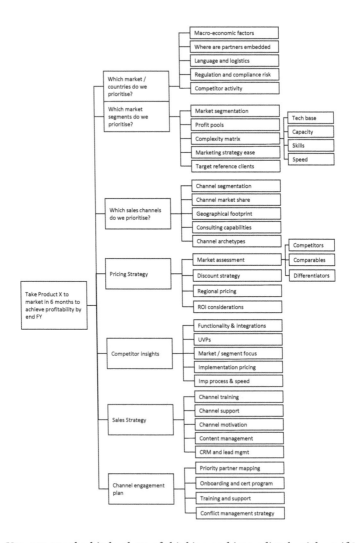

You can see the big buckets of thinking and immediately pick up if I have missed something. You can then go down each branch to see if any main elements are missing. There was a third layer, but I've omitted it (except for the one bit to show it's there) to fit everything on a page. This was done over the course of a couple of working sessions on Miro and it still lives there for reference years later.

Note: The issue tree is not a planning tool—it isn't "what do we have to do?" The issue tree is "what should we think about?" We are diverging and covering the whole problem. If you aren't sure if it should be there then put it on the tree! Even "obvious" stuff that you won't do. Put it on. It might trigger thinking on stuff that is important. Our next step is prioritization—don't start it too early.

Prioritize the focus areas

Once you have your head(s) around the problem and you've given due diligence to strategically diverging, it's time to prune the tree and decide what to take forward to be analyzed. Here, the focus is generally impact and ease of capturing impact—a classic two-by-two matrix:

Don't work to the nth degree to determine impact—quick-and-dirty, back-of-the-envelope calculations will help you get a good initial view of your matrix. Use the team, preferably in an engaging way from the **Manage Synergy** section, to seek your most directionally accurate view.

Work planning

This is by far the most neglected step in management and problem solving. And let me give you an example of why this is a problem:

In a meeting, an executive says to the business development manager: *I heard that MDX is aggressively targeting Canada. Will you please look into that for our next session?*

Four weeks pass and the team enters their next business development review session.

First on the agenda is "Review of Canada as a Strategic Target." The slide count at the bottom of the screen says "1 of 82" slides. It becomes clear that the BDM and their team has spent the better part of two weeks deeply interrogating Canada as a business development target.

All the executive expected was a couple of phone calls to their Canadian contacts to get a quick read on what was happening on the ground.

This is where work planning comes into its own.

> **WORK PLANNING SHOULD BE CALLED "WORK EXPECTATION SETTING"**

If I want the two-hour answer, I'll tell my team to spend no more than an hour on the question. If I want a few quick phone calls, I will tell my team to make a few quick phone calls. Parkinson's Law states that: **work expands to fill the time allocated to it.** Great executives never forget that. Yes, a workplan may be out of date in a couple of days as things change and learnings are incorporated. But proactively managing the team's expectations on how they spend their precious time and attention is fundamental to productivity.

Analysis

Step 5 is the one we are all familiar with: do the research, have the interviews, build the model, run a focus group. Whatever it is, here we are deep diving into the priority elements of the problem in line with how we have agreed to plan our work.

Synthesis

As we complete our analyses, we ask the question: "So what?"

What do we do with these results? What insights are they giving us? What actions could we take? How do they relate to other insights we have gained to build a strategic picture?

Recommendations and action plans

Last, we structure all our insights into a holistic strategy, concrete actions plans and compelling communications to move everyone in the desired direction.

I've been in enough meetings where managers are taking me for a tour of what they have learned, what's broken, and what they have researched without telling me what they want to do with the learnings.

> "FOOD FOR THOUGHT" IS THE ENEMY OF SYNTHESIS. AS A MANAGER, YOU'RE PAID TO CONSUME THE FOOD, ADD THE THOUGHT, AND COME BACK WITH RECOMMENDATIONS AND ACTION PLANS.

The seven-step problem-solving process is a McKinsey classic. Obviously, it is best suited to strategic problem solving. Whiteboarding a problem statement worksheet with your office manager when the printer stops working won't be the best use of anyone's time. It takes practice to do well and, eventually, becomes second nature when orchestrating problem solving.

> HAVING AN EXPLICIT PROBLEM-SOLVING APPROACH, KNOWING WHERE THE TEAM IS IN THE PROCESS, AND ENSURING EACH STEP IS GIVEN ITS DUE CARE AND DILIGENCE WILL MAKE YOU A BETTER STRATEGIC PROBLEM-SOLVING LEADER.

Design thinking[11]

For discrete problem solving the human-centered design process from the Stanford Design School is a great framework. Whether it is solving a customer problem, or improving a user experience, the Stanford d.school process is a good one.

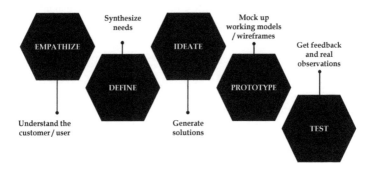

Overall, it has two diverge and converge flows.

Empathize – diverge

Define – converge

Ideate – diverge

Prototype and Test – converge

Empathize: It starts with getting into the minds and needs of your customers. What is the base line? How are things done now? What do they know they need or how do they want to feel?

Analyzing and generating a baseline customer journey map is very helpful to understand the rational and emotional pain points.

Define: This is a key interim convergence point to synthesize our empathizing into defined pain points and key success factors. Even if a customer "knows" what they want, that may not be the optimal,

---

[11] Learn much more at https://dschool.stanford.edu/resources/getting-started-with-design-thinking

or most innovative solution. Isolating what the core issues are as a foundation is similar to "problem definition" in the seven steps, but this starts with a very customer or audience centric approach. On the following page is an example of a customer journey (and emotional rollercoaster) we mapped for the car-buying process.

Ideate: Brainstorming possible solutions to the core problems. Imagining what an ideal customer journey would be. Engagement with customers, focus groups, parallel use cases/industries to come up with ideas.

Prototype: Creating quick-and-dirty mock-ups to try out. Wire-framing, role-playing, rapidly iterating to get an 80/20 solution out. Deliberately failing-forward with a "sticky-tape" and chewing gum working model.

Test: A more structured real-life trial of the potential solution. More deliberate testing with structured feedback and deep review of iterations. Clearly understanding impediments to incorporate into further iterations along the process.

As is customer journey

Jessica has a new job as a medical rep and is looking for a fuel-efficient car. She will get a $2,000 a month car allowance. Jessica knows very little about the technical aspects of cars.

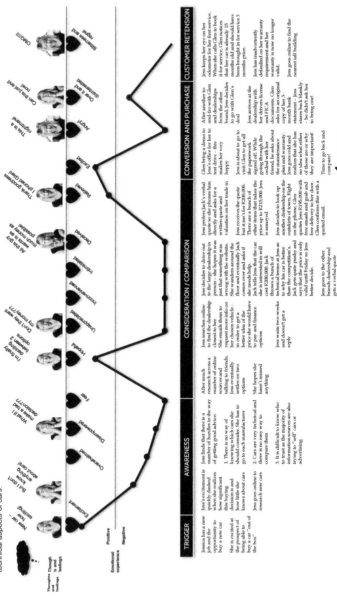

	TRIGGER	AWARENESS	CONSIDERATION / COMPARISON	CONVERSION AND PURCHASE	CUSTOMER RETENTION
	Jessica has a new job and the opportunity to buy a new car	Jess finds that there is a number of hurdles in the way of getting good advice:	Jess searches online to find the dealership closest to her	Jess prefers Jack's verbal quote so she phones him directly and asks for a written quote and valuation on her trade in	After another to-and-fro with Glen and dealerships from the other brand, Jess decides to go with Glen's deal
	She is excited at the prospect of being able to buy a car "out of the box"	1. There is no way of knowing which cars she should consider. She has to go to each manufacturer	She emails them to request more info on her chosen vehicle in order to get a better idea of the price she would have to pay and finance options	Jess receives the quote but it isn't for R200,000. There are a bunch of other items that takes the price up to R215,000. Jess is annoyed	Jess arrives at the dealership to sign her drivers license and FICA documents. Glen asks for an original copy of her 3-month bank statement – Jess stares back blankly – he didn't ask her to bring one!
	Jess goes online to research new cars	2. Cars are very technical and there is no easy way to compare them	Jess searches online to find the dealership closest to her		
		3. It is difficult to know who to trust as the majority of information sources are also trying to "sell" cars or advertising	Jess decides to drive out to the large dealership in person – she hopes it was just that something was wrong with the website. She wanders around the floor and eventually Jack comes over and asks if she needs help.	Jess decides to look up another dealership on the outskirts of town. Right on the phone Glen quotes Jess R195,000 with free smash and grab and free delivery to her door. Glen confirms this with a quoted email.	Jess keeps her eye on her odometer for her first service. When she calls Glen to book it for service, Glen notices that her car is already 15 months old and should have been brought in for service 3 months prior.
		After much research across a number of online sources and talking to friends, Jess eventually settles on two options	Jack tells Jess that the car she is interested in will cost R200,000. Jack throws a bunch of technical terms at Jess as to why his car is better than the competition's. Jack gets quite pushy and says that the price is only valid until Friday so Jess better decide.	Glen bring a demo to Jess's office for her to test drive – this makes her very happy	Jess has inadvertently defaulted on her warranty requirement and her warranty is now no longer valid.
		She hopes she hasn't missed anything	Jess goes to the other brands dealership and gets a verbal quote	Jess is about to go to visit Glen to get all the paperwork signed off. While going through the ordeal with her friend, he asks about the maintenance plan and warranty. Jess goes cold and realizes that she has no idea what either of those are or why they are important	Jess goes online to find the nearest tall building
			Jess waits two weeks and doesn't get a reply	Time to go back and compare!	

Thoughts and feelings

Emotional experience — Positive / Negative

Human-centered design and the d.school process is a great framework for discrete problem solving. There are a lot of parallels with the d.school process and Agile project management/software development.

The key caution point is not to short-circuit the process. It's very easy to interview a couple of customers, jot down what they want, and then go away and build it. While this may solve problems, it doesn't push the thinking to identify innovative and groundbreaking solutions.

And sometimes you don't need these. So, use your executive manager mind to decide whether you just need to solve problems or need to expend more energy pushing boundaries and innovating.

The Five Whys

This popped up in some OKR work I was doing recently.

We had identified an issue with two systems that weren't adequately talking to one another. System 1 was an ops system that was used to capture information in a process. This information was transferred to system 2 for reporting purposes.

The problem was that system 1 couldn't be locked. So, as expected, there were no inherent change controls for how that information was handled. And ops need to change stuff as a default part of their operations.

This created endless issues for users of system 2 because the data was always "wrong" and, hence, they were always "wrong." But it wasn't their fault.

A key result for the team to work on was the rectification of the change control process. A second key result was to get the systems better integrated to manage changes more automatically and escalate issues. Those were two good next steps. But they were not root causes. I was interested in three things:

> · *Who had designed the process and systems to allow these obvious gaps to exist in operations?*
>
> · *Who was responsible for the systems deployments and integrations, and how could a system go live with these risks?*
>
> · *Why wasn't this proactively raised and proactively managed by the management team?*

Once we started asking around, it turned out that there were a number of other, similar examples in other systems. This pointed to a root cause in project and IT processes that needed to be more systemically fixed.

How did we get there? We asked the Five Whys.

Almost 100 years old, the Five Whys originated in industrial manufacturing and is attributed to the founder of Toyota, Sakichi Toyoda.

The premise is simple: keep asking "why?" until you have uncovered sufficient root causes. Is it five? Three? Seven? Eleven? Doesn't matter. Five is a good guide but keep asking until your executive brain is happy.

System 2 sometimes doesn't match system 1 which causes issues in reporting.

Why?

System 2 pulls from system 1 once but operations changes system 1.

Why?

They need to and there aren't change controls between the systems.

Why?

We need an ongoing sync between the systems to identify changes and escalate issues in the reports already published. When it was deployed, it wasn't catered for.

Why?

There wasn't enough customer engagement in the project process and deadline rigidity incentivized the IT team to deploy whatever they could to appear "successful."

Why?

Our broader project processes are not designed to be customer centric, and the project plans, specs and outcomes are not signed off by the customers who use them.

Done! Root cause identified. Strategic project initiated.

It is deceptively simple, like all good frameworks.

And it becomes a way of executive thinking. But I do find myself having to remind my managers about it. Especially when it comes to identifying cross-functional dependencies and flow on issues.

Keep the Five Whys in your back pocket.

Back to strategic problem solving

Now that we have explored three very different approaches to different problem solving, let's come back to the word "strategic." Remember what we said earlier about time, focus and attention being a finite resource?

NOT EVERY PROBLEM NEEDS A SOLUTION.

And certainly not a groundbreaking innovative and resource consuming one.

Sometimes you need to put a band-aid on something. Sometimes you want to stop at the second "Why?" and just solve that. Do not fall into the trap of thinking every improvement opportunity is a good one.

USE YOUR EXECUTIVE MANAGER MINDSET TO FOCUS PROBLEM SOLVING FOCUS AND ATTENTION ON WHERE THEY ARE GOING TO MOVE THE NEEDLE.

REPORTING STRATEGIC PROGRESS AND MANAGING UP

By the time one reaches executive levels, it has become second nature to "manage up" and show the relevant key stakeholders what is happening in the business and your portfolio.

As a manager and executive, you are entrusted with a part of the business to run and manage to generate value for shareholders.

At executive level, comprehensive board reports and financials are routinely generated to let stakeholders know where the business stands and to proactively manage expectations on performance.

Trust is equally as important at a business level as it is at a personal level. Shareholders have provided necessary investments into the business for it to operate, add value, grow, and increase in value. Shareholders want reliable performance against expectations. No surprises.

You can imagine how the market would feel about a listed company that suddenly reports earnings 40% below expectations. This lack of reliability creates mistrust, and the market will take their money elsewhere.

Imagine the same scenario where the market expected a poor results announcement but had clarity on why and what the executive team was doing to address it and exceed expectations going forward.

This same mindset should happen at all levels of business.

Now that you have OKRs in place, you are tracking key results, KPIs and activities to make OKRs happen; you are problem solving to identify root causes of issues; you are in a very good place to proactively report upwards and show the value of what you are doing. Add in strategic thinking in updated narratives, functional strategies, and SCRs and you'll be on your way to the boardroom in no time.

> YOU ARE NOT SHOWING OFF. YOU ARE GIVING YOUR LEADER WHAT THEY NEED TO KNOW AND SHOWING THAT YOUR SPACE IS IN TIP TOP CONDITION.

Another significant development opportunity in terms of "reporting upwards" and showing off what you are doing is collaborating with your line leader to understand what they want to know about. This is a great opportunity to check in and get into the mind of your leader and what they are interested in and worried about:

> *Hey Tom. I am reviewing my regular reporting to make sure that it is on point and holistic. To provide you and the management team with information and updates that are succinct and insightful, I would like to set up a session to discuss:*
>
> - *What do **you** need to report upwards in terms of my function?*
> - *What's keeping you up at night that I can proactively update you on?*
> - *I would like to align on the five KPIs that matter most and provide these in dashboard format so that you have them at your fingertips. I'll bring industry best practices for us to refer to.*
> - *Over and above reporting on the strategic priorities in my OKRs, is there anything else that is of specific interest to the leadership team and executives?*
> - *I'll be sure to continue including any insightful outputs like our functional strategy review document and recent values survey. We can check in on these monthly to make sure I'm forwarding you good stuff to show off with the executives.*

Most importantly, do your homework. What are the routine things that are tracked in a department like yours? What do good dashboards look like?

DON'T WAIT TO BE ASKED FOR INFORMATION. PROACTIVELY PROVIDE IT IN INSIGHTFUL, SUCCINCT, AND EASY TO UNDERSTAND FORMATS THAT SHOW YOU ARE NOT ONLY PERFORMING BUT ARE REPORTING AT AN EXECUTIVE MANAGER LEVEL.

Remember, being secretive or obscure about what you are doing, and the quality of your department's outputs, creates anxiety and doubt, which destroys trust and is career limiting.

Managing up

We know that time, focus and attention are scarce resources. But what do we do when our leaders are asking for more and more, adding more and more to our plates or coming up with "good ideas" that we don't think are good ideas?

We all wish our bosses were rational but often they aren't.

FIRST AND FOREMOST, BE VERY CLEAR ABOUT WHAT IS BEING ASKED FOR.

I have seen numerous managers freak out about something that has been asked for, but they have the ask all wrong.

- Is the executive asking for a two-hour answer, or a two-week investment?
- The executive mentioned this as an idea. Are they emotionally attached to it? Did they expect me to implement it? Or were they just thinking out loud?
- Given I'm uncomfortable and surprised by the ask, am I sure I'm on the right track and not misunderstanding it?

Before freaking out, proactively ask for clarification:

Hey Tom. You asked for a view on Canada as a sales opportunity. My team is flat out at the moment with OKR1 and OKR2, so I just wanted to clarify next steps so I can move forward effectively. Doing A will give us a good sense of whether this is a tree worth barking up. If we were to do B or C, then we would have to wait for capacity to free up or reprioritize OKR 1 or OKR 2.

My overall advice is to be clear and transparent about what is on your plate. Too many times I have seen managers and leaders go head-to-head about capacity and what's possible while having to read each other's minds.

IN MIND-READING COMPETITIONS, THE SENIOR LEADER ALWAYS WINS. NEVER LEAVE IT TO MIND READING.

The health of your OKRs and BAU[12] KPIs are the first half of your secret weapon.

If you are struggling to finish strategic projects and there are red markers on your monthly KR check-ins and quarterly OKR check-in, then clearly you don't have capacity to take more on. If leadership wants to put more on, what balls are they happy for you to drop, or what needs to be re-prioritized?

Get stuff down on paper.

Go back to your OKRs and OKR health checks. Update your issue trees. Build out a workplan to roughly map out where time and focus is being spent. Through this process, you may discover a way to meet in the middle.

If after all of this, you still feel like it's a "no" in your mind.

DON'T GO BACK WITH A "NO", GO BACK WITH A "HELP!"

Flesh out the problem solving.

Have a "I need help to figure this out" working session to revisit all the above. Do some Five Whys. Paint out the scenarios. Revisit the workplan and see what's possible by making some workstreams more condensed or by dividing and conquering. Maybe you are missing something, and it is a good idea? Maybe you can fit it in? If not, you have a well thought out plan with which to go back and say *Help!*

Last, get a group together.

If you still think that you don't have capacity, or an idea is a bad one, set up a project meeting with a good group of stakeholders. This meeting is not called "Why is Tom's idea a bad one?" This meeting is called the "group working session on how to get Tom's idea done with everything else we are doing." This way you are bringing all the structured thinking to the table and can get help from others to weigh in on and break the stalemate.

---

[12] Business as usual

Through all of this, it is worth thinking through your onstage and back-stage management strategy. This leads us onto **managing staff**, where we will get into this executive thinking technique in more detail.

MANAGE STRATEGY TO-DO LIST

☐ Craft your strategic narrative using the SCR framework. Collaborate with your boss. Communicate it to your team.

☐ Craft your team vision, mission and values with your managers and team members. Incorporate scenario thinking. Develop associated OKRs for yourself and your team members.

☐ Build a problem statement worksheet for a strategic project even if it's already on the go. Build the issue tree—double check you aren't missing any key aspect. Think about how you have managed work expectations on the major tasks currently being undertaken.

☐ Apply human-centered design thinking to a problem and ask the Five Whys.

☐ Build an executive dashboard for your boss to show your portfolio is under control.

MANAGE STAFF

"Strategy without execution is useless.
Execution without strategy is aimless."

−JOHN KOTTER, HARVARD BUSINESS SCHOOL PROFESSOR AND AUTHOR

T HE ROLE OF A MANAGER IS TO KEEP PEOPLE ON TRACK. If we consider a train, we would be a pretty poor transport company if our strategy for keeping our train on track was to pick it up and put it back on the track, as quickly as possible, every time it fell off. Most managers and executives I have worked with expend inordinate amounts of energy picking up trains and dealing with the frustration of them derailing more often than needed. Addressing this comes down to being proactive in your management approach.

Stopping trains from derailing takes good ground, good tracks, good signals, good teams, good systems, good planning and good driving. The sooner you start, the sooner you'll get there.

I totally appreciate that you aren't starting with a blank canvas here. And nothing about executive thinking is linear or "paint-by-number." So, grapple with the thinking and take some new perspectives with you to take advantage of opportunities as they present themselves.

Recruiting is the front of our funnel. Having the right team members onboard is fundamental. We start our journey by being deliberate about who we are putting into play—how we identify gaps, how we find talent, and how we onboard them effectively.

Once we have all the members, we need to conduct the trains. We explore how to set up an effective management operating system and how to spend your time as an executive manager. We then run through how to think about engaging with your team members to get them mastering their roles and responsibilities. We leverage what we have already built in the **manage strategy** section and explore tough conversations.

As a conductor, we don't do all our leading, coaching and managing from the control tower. We manage on stage and backstage to get things done.

Last, we discuss stress and resilience—a fundamental part of every job.

THE ROLE OF A MANAGER

A manager is the custodian of a part of the business. As the custodian, the manager is responsible for coordinating their people, processes and systems to deliver quality outcomes, in line with the business strategy, and sustainably.

Sustainably includes enabling your people to be successful and fulfilled. Being successful this month by burning your people out, doesn't make us successful next month. We need sustainable business and people.

The three main components in any manager's arsenal are people, processes and systems. Whenever assessing core competencies, bottlenecks, improvement opportunities, investments, anything to do with your business, consider this whole operational ecosystem.

As we have discussed before, a good manager doesn't need to know everything about their business to be effective. A great executive manager knows how to manage those with specialist knowledge, knows when to trust them, and knows when to get other opinions and support.

The power of networks

Great executive managers know how to leverage a network. There is only so much you are going to get from desktop/Google research and AI[13]. Sometimes it's best to seek out and engage someone who has been in a similar situation as you and ask them, *what do you wish you had known?* Having a thought partner to help you take practical learnings and apply them to your context is invaluable. While there are some consultants out there who may be helpful, I have yet to come across someone who hasn't helped me when I have asked for advice.

I have literally cold-called numerous people and said: *Hey, this is me.*

---

[13] There are some very good, practical, online resources out there, like *First Round Review.*

I can see/have heard that you have been through a similar situation. I could really use your advice. Can I buy you a coffee? Most people fundamentally like being helpful.

Grappling with what CRM system to invest in? Look through your network and see who knows someone who may use or know something about CRM systems in a line of work similar to yours. Ask for an e-introduction. Draft the email. Or just message them directly.

I've helped a lot of people on a lot of topics. I know what I'm good at, I know my boundaries and I know what I am willing to give away free to be helpful. If people don't ask me for help, I don't know that they need help.

ASK FOR ADVICE. WHAT'S THE WORST THAT CAN HAPPEN? I SAY, "SORRY—I'M TOO BUSY."

Networking isn't selling. I think a lot of people get intimidated by networking because they have a subconscious belief that networking is about "winning people over". It isn't. Networking is selfish. And everyone at a networking event, conference, seminar, webinar is selfish. The whole point of going to a conference is to learn new approaches and find new solutions to your problems. Just like everyone else. So, approaching networking with a two-pronged strategy helps:

· What am I trying to solve/figure out/learn?

· What do I know and what experience do I have that I can offer? No matter who is in the room, they have not got your experience. They have not tackled the exact problems and issues you have had. Know that and own that.

Hi, I'm Tom. I've run a couple of startups across three industries. I'm here to compare notes with other operational leaders while I'm trying to find a solution to intermediate management development. What do you do and what's currently keeping you up at night?

I'm not an extrovert. But I have problems to solve. Problems that other business leaders may have solved, so I might as well ask them.

Be the umbrella

The role of a manager includes running their business, improving their business and **protecting their business**. I have seen a lot of situations where a team is burned out, stressed out and at risk because their manager has been a funnel and not an umbrella.

Todd Jackson, former Gmail product manager, is credited with the analogy. And, like Tod, I'm sure we all know a funnel or two.

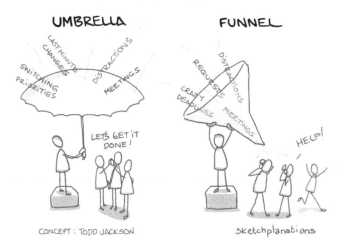

TWO POSSIBLE MANAGEMENT STYLES

UMBRELLA FUNNEL

CONCEPT : TODD JACKSON   sketchplanations

A big part of being a good executive manager is having courage and being able to manage up and out to protect the team.

> ENERGY, FOCUS, AND ATTENTION ARE FINITE RESOURCES, AND YOUR MANAGEMENT UMBRELLA PROTECTS THEM.

Thankfully, with your strategic narrative, OKRs and executive problem-solving skills, your umbrella has a solid foundation.

We will explore how to keep what's under the umbrella in order and then build more into the canopy in **Manage Synergy**.

ORGANIZATIONAL STRUCTURE

Again, we seldom get the chance to start with a blank canvas. And even when we do (like in a startup), there are so many unknowns that designing and building a perfect team is highly theoretical. However, having a structured view of where we are and where we are going is critical to build for future success.

We start with our strategy and strategic narrative. People and people strategy are intricately linked to how we got here—our wins and our losses. Intricately linked to where we are going and how we will deal with surprises along the way is our people and people strategy.

The first step in proactively managing your organization is ensuring you have the right organizational structure to support your strategy. You need to check that you have the right roles, at the right levels, and that the way they formally, and informally, interact with each other support your desired outcomes.

I have seen a lot of good strategies hampered because organizational designs undermine the needed behavior.

Focus, collaboration, silos, politics are all realities we need to cater for. Setting up the right structures up front will help you be more deliberate about containing or controlling them.

Even if you have a well-ingrained structure, question it and understand it for what it is. Leverage scenario thinking. Know what best practice looks like. Know what old practice looks like—how did sales organizations look? What were those pros and cons?

Even if you aren't restructuring an organization, it evolves. And you want to evolve it deliberately and in the right direction.

A couple of key pointers on organizational structure:

- Make sure accountability rolls up into the right roles. Specifically, you want to look at a structure and be able to see who is the point person for delivery in this department or function. This role needs to be accountable for the running, the changing and the complying of the function!

- Make sure peripheral structures don't undermine this accountability.

- Where this role needs to interface with other areas of the business, make sure these structures are set up to complement and not undermine.

If this seems abstract, it is. Organizational structures are complicated and depend on the function and strategic organizational design. Let me run through a quick example:

I was working with the regional sales division of a large, global organization undergoing a vital tech transformation to clean up and move to a cloud-based CRM. While this was vital and valuable to the business and sales VP, the project was a nightmare.

The tech projects were being run out of a central "technology" function.

The regional sales VP was busy running his business. The prototypes and iterations of the new system their sales team members kept testing was dismal. The tech function didn't have a good view of what the regional sales teams needed, or how they differed, and their priority KPI was to meet their roll-out deadline. His team had pointed out these obvious issues and were becoming disheartened—not only was the process obviously very inefficient, but they were also worried that the end product would be poor. The VP was escalating these issues to the central team.

The global team saw all of this and felt the regional VP needed to change his processes to fit the system. The VP felt the projects team needed to change the system to suit how they sold to customers in their region.

This dilution of accountability was creating a mountain of inefficiency, bad blood between the departments and general cultural problems. But the teams on the ground were just doing what they were told.

The answer: fix the org structure. The central tech team needed to conceive and plan the macro project from a global level. Then, the regional sales VPs needed their own project teams (reporting to them), to work closely with their sales managers, to customize the system and implement an effective solution.

Project conception: *Central tech needed accountability to conceive, point of contact, and identify a solution in collaboration with all the regional VPs. The regional VPs were key customers in this step of the process.*

Project implementation: *Then the regional VPs needed the accountability, resources and structure to be responsible to implement the system effectively. Central tech needed to play a consulting role on standardization and sharing best practices. But the ultimate responsibility for adopting the system to unlock efficiencies and sales productivity lay with the regional VPs.*

Some of this needed a structural fix, some needed an a responsible; accountable; consulted and informed fix, and some needed a process fix. Trying to fix the RACI and processes without the regional projects resources reporting to the regional VP would have been futile.

Organizational design is an art. And there is never a "right answer." Every structure/scenario has its own pros and cons. It's important to weigh them up, be very clear and aware of their pros and cons and try to cater to these in your RACIs and processes.

I've worked in many big organizations that deliberately change their macro-organizational design every four to five years to receive the benefits of the "other" design and keep people on their toes. An example of this would be to change from a product-led view (marketing, sales, distribution, and manufacturing teams set up and managed under the

Bud Light executive) to a functional centric design that has a sales function for all brands managed under one "sales exec" and then change back five years later.

Yes, good boards do think that far ahead.

EXECUTIVE HEATMAPPING

To gain an overall handle on how we are managing our function/business to take our strategic narrative forward, we need to objectively know how we are doing. I use an executive heatmap for this.

The heatmap

Take all the functions in your space—even gaps/empty ones—and put them across the top of a page.

Then, as a row, place your different levels of staff, processes, systems and any other cross-cutting core competencies you want to heatmap.

Then rate each block. I have included an example of one of my one pager executive heatmaps for reference.

Note, I use Harvey Balls[14]—with definitions that I find useful and intuitive (see example on the next page). Having a whole page of amber dots doesn't help anyone.

> **AN EFFECTIVE HEATMAP SHOULD GIVE YOU CLEAR GUIDANCE ON WHERE YOU SHOULD WORRY AND WHERE YOU SHOULDN'T.**

A full Harvey Ball never equals "best in the world." That's a pointless measure. Good enough to be effective and not have to worry about for the foreseeable future is a great shade of green in my books.

---

[14] Harvey Balls are round ideograms used for visual communication of qualitative information. They are commonly used in comparison tables to indicate the degree to which a particular item meets a particular criterion. **https://en.wikipedia.org/wiki/Harvey_balls**

Legend:
- ○ No resource; no function
- ◔ Ineffectively resourced
- ◑ Functioning with basic gaps
- ◕ Functioning; enroute to sustainability
- ● Effective, sustainable functionality

Matrix rows: Executive, Senior Mgmt, Middle Mgmt, Frontline staffing, Client Insights, Processes, Systems, Comments

Matrix columns: Brand, Marketing, Sales, Cust Support, Collect, Support 2, Claims, Partners, Projects, IT Infra, IT Development, MIS, Bus Intel and Analysis, Product Innov., Finance, HR

Comments:

Brand: Recent Brand Strategy launched and underway. Potential move to Head of Brand and Head of Direct Campaign Management without an Exec role over both

Marketing: Need a Campaign Management customofsm at the Snr Mgmt level. 2.0 in steady state. Focus on continuous improvement

Cust Support / Collect / Support 2 / Claims: Operations Manager needed. Improved CRM system required for client management, staff management and reporting

Partners: This function will need senior staffing and structuring if distribution strategy requires greater agent / broker presence

Projects: Require a replacement for Mohit and Senior Project Associates to run high value projects

IT Infra: Senior Infra Mgmt gap needs to be filled

IT Development: Senior Business Analyst required to round out team

MIS: Management capacity / skills need investment. Exec level oversight gaps. Potential need for CIO role to house Dev, MIS, BI and BA

Bus Intel and Analysis: Reporting to OD due to lack of CIO capacity

Product Innov.: Senior level "Product Executive" role vacant. Product innovation Associate and Product Analytics Associates roles being resourced and shaped in Q1

Finance: Potential book keeper. SA Finance Director position required

HR: HR Manager straddling middle and senior management roles

Looking at the heatmap example, you can see a couple of things quite intuitively:

- functional gaps where the entire column is blank—partner management and focused product innovation.

- clear leadership gaps at different levels depending on the function—this doesn't show any particular under investment trend in intermediate management, but rather evolutionary outcomes.

- a universal gap in customer insights across functions—something that may be worth investing in as a center of excellence to help empower the lines.

- core systems are looking good. Some investment in secondary systems is needed.

- processes are generally good and not cause for concern in core business areas.

An executive heatmap is a powerful analytical tool, and a powerful communication and collaboration tool to use with your leadership and management team.

BUILDING YOUR TEAM

The who

Now that we have our heatmap, we can turn our attention to how we are staffing and managing the people roles. I tackle this with three key lenses:

- **Do I have the right capacity?** Do I have enough of this? Do I need one person, two people or five people to adequately get this done and not burn anyone out?

- **Do I have the right level of skill?** Are the roles I have at the right level of seniority and experience? Do we have the right hard/technical skills? Do we have the right management and people skills? To what degree are our current team members "teachable" and ready to take on more complex roles and responsibilities when we need them?

> **IN MY EXPERIENCE, IF I HAVE THE RIGHT PROFILE, WITH GOOD INTRINSIC SKILLS AND CHARACTERISTICS, I CAN TRAIN THEM TO DO ANYTHING.**

This reminds me of Nicole:

> *I met my wife skydiving. That is a different story, but what matters in this context is that we spent many weekends out of town at the skydiving drop zone. One Saturday evening, I noticed a young woman sitting at the bar by herself. The skydiving community is a small one and a lonely, single visitor to the drop zone after dark is pretty unusual. I went over to introduce myself—to make friends and include this visitor into our weird community. Her name was Nicole.*
>
> *Nicole had just moved out of the city and was having a quarter-life crisis. We had a long chat (as I had had many quarter-life crises before) and we swapped notes. We became friends. It wasn't long before Nicole got involved in running operations at the drop zone: Organizing who was on which skydiving run and looking after the pilots. Eventually, Nicole was leading the coordination of national skydiving competitions and cross border events. Nicole was great. She was always smiling, partied with us at night but was up at the crack of dawn and ran a smooth operation. And running a smooth operation with a bunch of skydivers is no easy feat!*
>
> *Parallel to all of this, I was in the middle of co-founding a new tech startup. Things took shape and we were looking to bring on our first employee—I knew exactly who that should be. I gave Nicole a call and asked her if it was time to leave the countryside once more and come back to building a career. The answer was a resounding "Yes!"*
>
> *Nicole was employee number one and her first day was spent sitting side by side with me and my fellow co-founders in an airline lounge that doubled as our office.*
>
> *Shortly after, we secured a small office space and had our shareholders around to see the sites and have a board meeting. We discussed our progress, and they enquired about the background and profile of our first employee.*

I commented: "Nicole is great. A real go-getter. She will roll up her sleeves and do whatever we need."

We walked back to the office, through the door and found Nicole on hands-and-knees vacuuming under the desks. "I just couldn't take it anymore!" she exclaimed.

Fast forward seven years and Nicole has worked her way from customer service consultant to financial adviser to training manager to project manager to executive of projects, IT and BI!

Great intrinsic abilities and teachability, coupled with strong leadership and opportunity, equals success.

- **Do we have the right culture?** Are the profiles in these roles (or those that we are looking for to fill these roles) in line with the values and behaviors we need to achieve and have fun? Are there any energy drains? Do the personalities match the work? Are there personalities with blind spots that are hampering the work?

With a staff complement of 20 plus, don't go and do this for everyone. We want to have a birds-eye-view across all our team members for management, coaching and development needs. But we want to be rigorous in assessing our key roles and our people leaders.

At the end of the day, you want to balance and make the right deliberate trade-offs, across the three factors above to effectively staff your team.

For existing roles and staff, this exercise should inform your management, development and support approach to your key staff. Similar to your management heatmap, we need to take a good hard look at who we have got and how we are setting them up for success. Nobody's perfect, so we need to ensure we are structurally catering for blind spots in our managers and key staff to get the most out of what we've got. As we staff up new roles or fill vacancies, we are looking at the team ecosystem as a whole—across capacity, skills and profiles—to build a high-performing team, overall.

Promoting or hiring externally?

This is an age-old question. And I see a surprising number of managers wanting to promote internally rather than hire externally. It is great to grow individuals and provide high performers with opportunities. But,

THIS IS A BUSINESS—NOT A CHARITY.

If you have assessed the elements above, along with your heatmap, and all roads lead to promoting Tom into this key role, then go for it.

If promoting Tom means that he has to learn new stuff and prove himself—this will take time and might fail. If your OKRs could be put at significant risk by this strategy, then look at other options. You may find a great, experienced candidate that can hit the ground running and give Tom some real apprenticeship opportunities to take on a more senior role faster.

But this strategy isn't without risk. You may find a more experienced person with bad habits, a bad attitude, or the wrong experience. Once you have been down this road a few times, you appreciate:

RATHER THE DEVIL YOU KNOW THAN THE DEVIL YOU DON'T.

There are no right or wrong answers. But there are wrong approaches and that is to jump to conclusions. As we learned in executive problem solving, we want to diverge before we converge. Test the market. Let Tom know that he is up for consideration, but you have tough choices to weigh up given his lack of real experience.

HEDGE YOUR BETS. IT'S GOOD TO HAVE OPTIONS ON THE TABLE. JUST BECAUSE THERE IS AN OPTION ON THE TABLE, DOESN'T MEAN YOU HAVE TO TAKE IT.

Staff the role for the evolutionary period of the function

Some people are good at **building** stuff.
Some people are good at **changing** stuff.
Some people are good at **running** stuff.

When you are hiring a key manager or staff member, be conscious of the context they are going to operate under. Runners don't cope well with drastic transformations. They also prefer to have the playbook handed to them rather than building a playbook from scratch. Don't get me wrong, I'm sure they can build a playbook if asked. But it will probably take too long, and probably won't be agile enough. Being thoughtful about the archetype of individual you are after is important. Then think about the questions, experiences and characteristics you would like to explore when searching for the right person.

Using personality profiles during interviews

I get asked about this all the time. And it's a tricky one. In many countries, using personality profiles as part of formal job interviews is illegal. Yes, there are accredited psychometric tests that can be used but I'm not sure how useful they would be and they cost a fortune.

My view: Understanding what characteristics you want in a role is important and you can draw off a personality profiling framework for that language of descriptors. However, personality profiling tests do not test for intelligence. And, you don't know how self-aware and developed the individual is. Just because they are an 8, doesn't mean they are a self-aware and self-managed 8. And most roles need a variety of complementary skills and characteristics that can't be packaged into one type. I would use them to expand your preparation and thinking but not as a screening tool.

So, by now you should have a good view of what you are looking for and where they will fit in. Time to start the search.

THE RECRUITING PROCESS

I promoted this to be a bigger section as I feel it is such an important part of making your marathon a worthwhile one. The recruiting process is effectively the front of your management funnel and bugger-ups here flow into years of downstream pain. How you go about finding skills is very industry and market dependent. But, having interviewed and employed hundreds of people, I can provide some thought starters and practical tips and tricks that may be of help.

Birds of a feather flock together

Personal references are really valuable. Good salespeople can identify other good salespeople. People with good values don't hang around with or refer people with bad values. Building and maintaining your own personal network is extremely valuable when it comes to recruiting. Always remember:

> YOU CAN REACH OUT TO A GOOD REFERRAL FOR MORE REFERRAL – THINK OF THE NETWORKING EFFECT.

Let's say I'm looking for a good senior software engineer. My friend used to work with Steven and says Steven walks on water. But Steven has just started a new role at Space X and wouldn't be in the market.

Great! I'm sure Steven has friends and colleagues and experience. He may not be in the market, but he may know someone good who is. Let's ask him! The worst he could say is "no." It's worth a text.

Be very clear on the priorities you are recruiting for

Some people love job descriptions. I find them as useless as a concrete parachute when it comes to recruiting. We saw how a good, synthesized strategic narrative can help us contextualize and add richness to why we are doing what we are doing and what the priorities are.

Take that concept with you when you are recruiting key roles. What are the context, the unknowns, the priorities? How do you give recruiters, your friends, your network and the candidates a rich flavor of what you are looking for? Bullet points won't cut it for key roles. Every time I have been asked for a job description, I have responded with a succinct, insightful five-minute phone conversation to clearly explain what I'm solving for and making sure my audience "gets it."

We find ourselves in x situation and are looking for y role to really push z.

They need the usual a, b and c tickets to play, but it's really important that they also bring e and f attitude—probably from experience doing p and q.

I'd rather take a person with k only, than a person with l and no k. Copy. Paste. Use.

Test for attitude and intrinsic skills that matter

Interviewing for priority characteristics and attitude is key. The interview process is a complex one as candidates need to sell themselves without coming across as inauthentic. There is also incentive for someone to bullshit you or expand the truth somewhat.

A good interview approach should test for all of this and get under the skin of the Curious > Skeptic > Cynic spectrum. If you can't trust the read on the candidate themselves, then do deep interviews with referees. This is especially important for senior roles where individuals are hired to be thought leaders. This is where approach to curiosity is fundamental to the success of the individual as a member of a senior team.

Different roles need different intrinsic skills. Yes, we all want software developers that are extroverts and the life of the party with Daniel Craig dress sense, but trade-offs need to be made. Priorities need to be set. Does this role require high analytical skills? How are we going to test that? Does it require creative visual skills and a high attention to formatting accuracy? How are we going to test that?

Here is a quick non-exhaustive list of some of the things that I have needed to test depending on role:

- Verbal reasoning
- Analytical reasoning
- Abstract reasoning
- Numerical and quantitative reasoning
- Critical thinking
- Spatial/visual reasoning

Do some research and make sure your interviewing technique adequately tests what you are looking for in intrinsic skills.

Do your own screening and interviews

I have, and have had, fantastic people and HR managers and staff. But there is no way that they have the interview "sixth sense" for key staff that I would as the manager of the space. It is unbelievably inefficient to get HR to screen resumes and do interviews for you. I can look at 100 resumes in 20 minutes and find five or fewer candidates I would interview. There is no way HR is that efficient and will pass on stuff I would ding. This wastes their time and my time. Worse, they may ding interesting candidates that I would rather interview.

Do. Not. Set. Up. One. Hour. Interviews. As. Standard.

I always send an initial email to any candidates with three questions:

- Why are you looking to leave/did you leave your current role?
- What are you looking for in your next chapter?

- What are you looking to earn (total guaranteed cost to company) and what is your desired incentive/bonus structure?

The answers to these questions are insightful because I can gauge structure, content, tone and effort. I can also see if their aspirations are outside of the level I am recruiting for. If I'm hiring an intermediate manager and Tom wants to be an executive, then I'm wasting time interviewing Tom; Tom's at the wrong grade.

Then, have a 30-minute exploratory coffee (virtual) if you aren't sure about someone. Sometimes less time is appropriate.

I CAN OFTEN TELL IN FIVE MINUTES WHETHER I WOULD BE ABLE TO WORK WITH SOMEONE OR NOT.

There is nothing worse than knowing this and then having to politely spend 55 minutes listening to the person try and sell themselves. You can cut it short, but you've set a one-hour expectation and have a recruiting brand to worry about. It is a small world. So just don't set it up to be an hour, or use email more effectively.

Interrogate references!

I rented a house once that had its pros and cons. But one thing for sure was that I wouldn't have bought it. There were too many fundamental things wrong with it that would have taken an absolute fortune to sort out—many of which I only knew from living in it. The house went up for sale. The buyer bought it. Can you imagine my utter shock that the buyer didn't think about chatting to me through the process? Now every time something needs to be addressed and Mr. Buyer is surprised and deflated, I can only sympathize so much.

WHO RENTED THIS RESOURCE BEFORE YOU? INTERVIEW THE PREVIOUS TENANT!

Candidates have their own perspectives, lenses and personalities. What I think of my manager, Tom, versus what *Tom* thinks of Tom is obviously different.

Referees often find my "reference checks" quite tough. Here are some of the questions I routinely ask:

[Tell the person you are not providing business or role context on purpose. You want to focus on their experience and business first.]

- What advice can you give me about managing Tom?
- On a scale of 0–10 how would you rate Tom? What would it have taken from Tom to be a 10? Would you hire Tom again? [Note: anything below 8 here is a red flag].
- How would you describe Tom's overall working style and work ethic?
- What is Tom really good at? What strengths does he bring to the broader team?
- What does Tom need to work on to further his career?
- Is Tom flexible? Talk about Tom's resilience.
- What are the specific areas you needed to keep an eye on and assist with?
- How much management and oversight does Tom need to do what he needs to do? What was your engagement frequency with him?
- Any instances where things went wrong and you should have been alerted earlier?
- What kinds of personalities get along with Tom?
- What kinds don't?
- When there were conflicts or issues around Tom that were escalated, what were they typically? Can you give me an example?
- How would you describe his management style? What kinds of people enjoy working under him? What kinds don't?
- What else do I need to know about Tom that we haven't already covered?

[Provide business and role context and trade-offs]

- Overall, would you recommend Tom for x role?

Case interviews

Business cases are a valuable tool to do some real problem solving in the interview. I use this as much as possible with two flavors:

Generic business case: You can put together your own hypothetical business case that walks through a scenario to unpack and solve a problem. This is a good approach because it allows you to cover different problem-solving elements more holistically. However, the context and reality are theoretical so there are those limitations. The benefit: over time, you can benchmark people against previous interviewees.

Real case: Get the candidate to work with you, on a whiteboard, to help you solve a real problem in the role and area that they are being interviewed for. Either a current problem or a big-hairy problem you solved in the recent past. Get on a whiteboard (virtual or in person) and unpack and solve the problem like you would if was this person's first week on the job.

Either way, make sure your case reflects the reasoning skills that you want to test.

Visual reasoning: Walk through and pull apart a user interface and look for improvement opportunities.

Abstract reasoning: Walk through a new product idea or service offering.

It's not easy to build a case, but investing time now in finding the right new hire will pay off dividends over their career chapter with you. You can find numerous case interview examples online. I suggest starting with examples from the websites of McKinsey & Co, Boston Consulting Group and Bain.

ONBOARDING AND RAMP-UP

There are three key aspects to onboarding and ramp-up that I want to highlight, over the usual transactional processes.

Induction

Drawing from my experiences running basic consulting readiness at McKinsey, my manager/senior hire induction programs generally span five to six business days and include:

- Introduction to the company: Context and history; vision, mission and values
- Introduction to the industry and how we see the industry
- Mind of the customer—pain points and what success looks like
- Introduction to core products and unique value propositions (UVPs)
- Overview of competitors and where we fit in/compete
- Personality profiling testing and introductory working session
- Problem-solving training and communication skills training (the frameworks that we subscribe to as a business)
- Top-down functional heatmap discussion and handover
- Strategy working session
- 100-day plan working session

Some of this is cohort-based and some of this is one-on-one. As far as possible, I get line managers to give induction training. For example, I'll have the marketing manager and product manager co-present the product, customer and UVP introductions.

Where possible, I'll co-facilitate. This allows my managers to get insight into my thinking about any and all topics from day one.

Develop their 100-day plan

Why 100 days? Three months is a solid time frame to work with for a tactical ramp-up plan.

When a new manager comes on board, you need to manage a couple of things closely. They should be able to:

- Learn stuff as fast as possible, but effectively
- Get to know the people as fast as possible and build trust
- Take the opportunity to shake things up and change things deliberately by balancing the two points above

Explicitly laying this out in a 100-day plan will help you balance the different elements and set expectations for how long your new manager should be in "receiving mode" before you expect them to start giving.

In induction, we flesh out the issue trees we need. As a baseline, this would include the elements of the functional strategy. Then I would add a couple of strategic problems that are critical. This lays the thinking out and allows the new manager to read my mind.

Then, for the 100-day plan, as a broad guideline:

Month 1: check-ins and problem solving around priority elements of the issue trees to start getting the manager's hands dirty with real, focused work. That is, to grapple with topics, explore context and people. Explore options and opportunities.

Month 2: we start converging and defining strategies and strategic projects and revising OKRs.

Month 3: hold project kickoffs with new the manager as lead; start to make changes and realign focus areas in the team.

Apprenticeship: strategic problem solving

Starting from the issue trees in the induction week, I like to spend the first three to six months with a new manager, doing the bulk of strategic problem solving together.

I generally start with functional strategy. Even if we have one and we like it, I would never just hand over a strategy to a new manager. It is very disempowering. Revising and rebuilding the strategy is good for you and your new manager. It gets them thinking in the right way, it gives them ownership of the process and outcome, and you may pick up more insights with fresh eyes and experience.

We work on a relevant overarching strategy framework for the function—including checking how others have tackled this. We then go through a collaborative review of the strategy, working through it together and then engaging other managers and execs along the process. It's a great way to get a new manager up to speed, collaborating with the team and doing strategic thinking *with* you. And you're collapsing the 3Es into on-the-job training and apprenticeship.

Example: Stacey's first Marketing Strategy

We mentioned Stacey's marketing strategy earlier. Stacey joined one of my startups to look after marketing. A large portion of my most successful hires have been people with great intrinsics and limited experience. Stacey was one of these. Considering her very limited real-life marketing experience, I started tackling the 3Es with her. Task 1: build a brand and marketing strategy.

Education: *I set up a session to take Stacey through my brand and marketing strategy framework. I had used it before. We unpacked the elements of the framework and how they could apply to different businesses and products.*

Exposure: *I walked Stacey through some examples of my prior work. We looked at actual brand and marketing strategies and I explained some of the challenges we faced, the key insights and the surprises.*

Experience: *I then left Stacey to start working. We aligned on which pieces to prioritize, and I set out enough time for her to cut her teeth* *on—without too much wheel spinning and frustration. I made it crystal clear that we* were co-creating it and that I wanted good drafts, good questions and good insights. And I wanted her to keep track of the process (balcony) not just do the doing (dance) so that she could run the process herself in future as a thought leader.

While there were different elements of the 3Es involved, they were seamless, and we went back and forth while she learned **on the job.**

You can see the difference here between micro-management and apprenticeship.

> AS SOON AS POSSIBLE IN OUR WORKING RELATIONSHIP, I WANT MY MANAGERS TO UNDERSTAND HOW I THINK AND I WANT TO UNDERSTAND HOW THEY THINK.

This is the foundation of effective and trust-based delegation.

By grappling with strategic problems together—from problem definition and issue tree to outcomes and recommendations—you gain deep insight into how each other thinks. You also find your problem-solving groove. *Where can your thinking complement mine and where will mine complement yours?*

Because I set this up as an ingoing expectation it cuts through ego, impostor syndrome, arrogance, etc.

Here we solve problems together. Together. We don't give proposals and shoot down proposals. We unpack problems and build solutions side by side.

Across hard strategy, people strategy, team dynamics, personal dynamics, career development, everything:

> I WILL NOT ASK A NEW MANAGER FOR A PROPOSAL IN THEIR FIRST SIX MONTHS. I'D BE SETTING THEM UP FOR FAILURE.

If you do the above effectively, you'll be getting 360-degree feedback that goes something like this (actual 360-degree feedback I received):

Moving into the next phase of the business, Tom will need to let out the reins a little with the management team and give them 51% of the vote.

While he is always going to need to be in the mix, it isn't sustainable to be giving direction all the time, so his team will need to have a level of autonomy and trust that they can have the decision-making mandate on certain things, and that they will live with the ups and downs of those calls.

This was six months into the ramp-up of a new startup management team. The training wheels were removed shortly after this.

Culture and how you work

In addition to the content, it is also important to onboard your managers to how you work: the behaviors, approaches and values that you operate under. My collaborative strategic problem-solving approach is one of them.

You can't "can" these into a PowerPoint slide. Much of these are observations and reflections on the job. This is true apprenticeship. Here is an example:

I was in my first startup, and we hired a new executive, Natalie. Two weeks in, Natalie had done some analysis and scheduled a meeting with me, and the CFO, to take me through the findings and recommendations. We sat down in the boardroom and Natalie projected her screen. She then proceeded to, word-for-word, read what was on the screen. And it was a comprehensive analysis, to be fair.

I knew where this was going, and I had a choice to make: I could either be polite and nod and smile and try not doze off while Natalie read to me. Or I could interrupt her. I interrupted her: "Sorry Natalie. I can read much faster than you can talk. Let's get to the 'so what' here." Natalie froze. The CFO froze. Hell froze. But Natalie got the message.

A couple of hours later, between meetings, I went looking for Natalie and pulled her into a meeting room. I explained: "I understand that that's the way you are used to having meetings, but we don't do that here. If you were a more junior staff member, I would have let you read on. But, as an executive, I want you fitting in and adding value and working effectively as soon as possible; so I pounced on the opportunity. I hope you understand that it's because I want you to be successful and a role model—even though you're a new executive here." She admitted that my approach was a bit unorthodox, but she got the point and appreciated the radical candor.

I got a call from Natalie eight years later. She was laughing hysterically. "You won't believe it," she said, between giggles, "I just had to tell someone that I can read faster than they can talk!"

Natalie and I have been close friends ever since that first meeting—and she hasn't read to anyone but her children since.

MANAGEMENT OPERATING SYSTEMS

Great Managers love systems thinking and mapping stuff out. But I've seen few apply this thinking to how they manage.

How you cascade information, share information, report information, plan, review progress, set priorities, problem solve, stay on course, change course is all part of your management operating system (MOS). The basis of your MOS is information flows and collaboration needs.

The different spheres of management

You need to juggle different business needs at different levels of abstraction. Often these get crossed, probably due to the lack of deep work.

When we are discussing strategy, vision and mission, we are actively engaging in abstract reasoning. We are imagining possibilities and looking outwards. We consider scenarios and join abstract dots to bring conclusions back to now.

This is very different from how our brains engage in analytical reasoning. Breaking down tangible relationships and processes, identifying bottlenecks, analyzing where responsibilities lie—this is very tangible critical thinking. And, in my experience, we don't change gears very quickly.

Yet, some managers will still try and discuss strategic topics in the same meeting as a short-term business performance review. And one of the topics suffers. I'm sure you have been in a meeting like this. It feels like one of the two isn't given sufficient justice and there is more to delve into. But somehow no one has the mental bandwidth, and they throw in the towel. This is getting levels of abstraction crossed.

As a manager, you have to manage at a:

- **Strategic level** (strategy, value propositions, competitive advantage, long-term org changes)
- **Tactical running level** (KPIs, key results, postmortems, budgets, targets, highs, lows)
- **Tactical changing level** (project meetings, operational problem solving and innovation, how to change the machine)

I would be very deliberate about having *different* meetings around these topics. Even if they are the same audience. And don't go from one into the other and split up the agenda. People need to change mental gears. This holds for business, process, technical and people problem solving.

AS YOU THINK THROUGH YOUR MOS, PAY ATTENTION TO EACH OF THE SPHERES: STRATEGIC, TACTICAL RUNNING AND TACTICAL CHANGING.

Some things can be shared via dashboards. Some things via email in narrative or qualitative form. Some things need to be talked about. Some don't.

1. The first step in developing an effective MOS is determining your planning horizons. For a typical function and department there are four horizons:

   · Annual strategy and budget reviews

   · Quarterly OKR reviews

   · Monthly performance reviews and priority setting

   · Weekly or fortnightly operations reviews and priority setting

2. As we discussed in **Manage Strategy**, we start by developing our strategy, OKRs and plans top-down and cascade this through the functions and departments.

3. We then start tracking performance on a weekly, fortnightly and monthly basis to see how we are doing against plan.

4. We then adjust our plans and priorities given the new information to proactively influence next month's performance.

5. Quarterly, we take stock of this process and how effective it is in delivering our BAU KPIs and OKRs. If there are significant structural roadblocks that will impact overall strategy, we may revise and adjust OKRs and cascade this down to be reflected in next quarter's plans.

6. Annually, we look at broader three- to five-year strategy and missions. Similarly, we take stock, apply lessons learned, adjust, cascade and plan accordingly.

The core of the MOS is week-to-week and month-to-month planning. This is where things get lost in the weeds and where "death by meetings" can occur.

A useful exercise in this respect is to run a collaborative MOS design process with your team members. Below is an example output of one of my sessions. ***Don't worry—you're not supposed to be able to read the details.*** Along the left and the top are the various functions we were concerned with. The brief was:

   · Left to right: I am Function x and I need to share this information with Function n

   · Top to bottom: I am Function x and I need to get this information from Function n

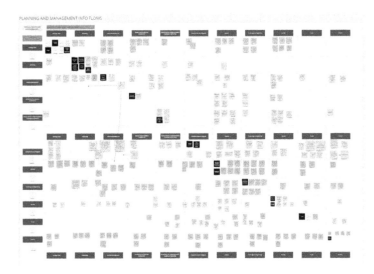

How doesn't feature yet. This was just a comprehensive view of all the information, insights, so-whats, and forward and backward thinking that needed to be shared.

Workshopping this was great as it gave an insightful and holistic view and allowed managers to explain to the broader group why certain information was important to them to perform their function. There were some interesting insights along the way.

So:

1. Define information requirements.

2. Cross off things that can be shared via existing dashboards and ensure access is granted.

3. Build dashboards for things that can be shared via dashboard but aren't in dashboard format yet.

4. Determine what can be shared via email, set the frequency and put recurring reminders in the calendar to make sure these are sent.

5. For collaborative information sharing, planning and problem solving, review, planning and working sessions are set up at the necessary frequency with clear purpose, participants, preparation, and process

to make them effective. Where possible, agendas are rolled together if the same audience is meeting at the same frequency.

Personally, I don't like to work with monthly beats because it creates odd weeks and clashes. I use a rolling four- or six-weekly beat to my MOS designs to keep calendars aligned.

Stepping back out of the details...

A DELIBERATE MOS GIVES YOU A PROACTIVE WAY TO MANAGE INFORMATION AND COLLABORATION TO ELIMINATE "MEETINGS FOR THE SAKE OF MEETINGS."

I like to revise my MOS every six months as a proactive hygiene check-in. We all have meetings that are painful and ineffective, but they have been around forever, have become part of the company culture, and everyone is scared to question why you're having it. Vaporizing your MOS every six months means that there are no sacred cows, and that you give the team equal right to question every meeting and interaction for its effectiveness.

I set up recurring meetings for 26-week cycles. When these end, it's time to look at whether the meeting was being effective before putting in another series.

Ideal diary

While you are developing and iterating your MOS you should also be defining your ideal diary. This is a deliberate view of how much time you should be spending on what, on a weekly, monthly and quarterly basis. There are two ways I like to do this:

· calendar view
· stacked bar

Calendar view

The concept behind an ideal diary is self-explanatory: without any distractions or surprises, what would your perfect week and month look like in your calendar?

This isn't only about meetings! This is about how you are spending your time. What are you spending it on and who with? Time, focus and attention are major currencies in the management world. Crafting our ideal diary, and managing it closely, gives us the most value for money. I start with an overarching intention of my week and what is most appropriate to work on and when:

- Reviews and plannings are better on Tuesdays and give my teams Monday to get their heads together.
- Broader coaching sessions and check-ins I like to do offsite over coffee or a glass of wine (virtual or in person) and Thursday afternoons are good for that. If I have six reports, and we have meaningful overall strategy, career, feedback and development check-ins once every six weeks, then that's one a week for me.
- I carve out time in my calendar to make sure I am reading about pertinent best practice and not being reactive. Friday mornings are good for that.

And so forth.

Once I have my week structured at a macro level, I can then put meetings in their desired bucket. My managers and project leaders know to schedule any project meetings on a Wednesday so as not to disrupt the MOS. My managers and others with direct reports know that Tuesday is their day to use me on BAU.

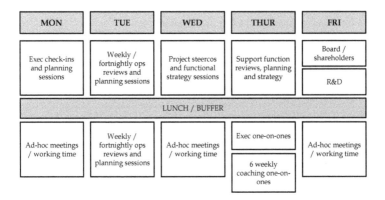

MON	TUE	WED	THUR	FRI
Exec check-ins and planning sessions	Weekly / fortnightly ops reviews and planning sessions	Project steercos and functional strategy sessions	Support function reviews, planning and strategy	Board / shareholders R&D
LUNCH / BUFFER				
Ad-hoc meetings / working time	Weekly / fortnightly ops reviews and planning sessions	Ad-hoc meetings / working time	Exec one-on-ones 6 weekly coaching one-on-ones	Ad-hoc meetings / working time

Stacked bar graph

Coming out of this, you can see a pretty good spread of how much time you are spending on what topic. As life goes on and things are disrupted, you may find the balance shift. Whenever I do a calendar intervention with a manager or executive, I always ask them to have a run through of their last couple of weeks and categorize how many hours they have spent on what in a typical week.

You want to make sure you are being deliberate on how much time you spend on:

· Planning

· BAU reviews and problem solving

· Time with your direct reports

· Career development and coaching time with your direct reports

· Proactive project management

· Reactive fire fighting

There are no rules. But if you build your stacked bar chart, and the hours you are spending on a category far outweigh what you or your boss would think appropriate (in hours and as a proportion of total hours), then you need to fix that.

Sometimes it is saying "no" to meetings.

Often, it's controlling what meetings are for.

Having a proactive MOS and deliberate MOS reviews can help you keep your ideal diary and the ideal diary of your managers in line with where you should be investing your time, focus and attention.

Your MOS is the structured, proactive approach to sharing information and engaging. If this backbone is strong, it will keep everyone in the loop on information pertinent to them, ensure effective collaboration where it is needed, and make the most use of time.

TRUST, CANDOR AND CRUCIAL CONVERSATIONS

No matter how proactive you are, or how good your MOS, a difficult conversation is inevitable. At some point as managers, we all have to discuss an issue, a development need, a cluster. Let's leave the standard grade feedback model behind and get to the executive thinking part.

Tough conversations are a long-term game. You need to be building up that emotional bank account, and laying the tough conversation foundation, long before the need arises. One of the worst ways to have a tough conversation is to never have tough conversations.

Being nice and positive and "a great boss" is only part of the job. Like in any relationship, if you sweep the small things under the rug, you start creating a mound that the rug will eventually slide off. A buildup of issues—coupled with the lack of practice between you and this person to resolve conflict—can result in a catastrophe.

Start easing into difficult conversation early. It doesn't have to be around specific issues or the need for anyone to change. It just creates comfort that you can hold a safe space for hard things to be discussed. Many poor managers simply don't have the emotional bandwidth to do this. Show that you're different.

TOP TIP: ADMIT YOUR FAULTS FIRST. ROLE MODEL TALKING ABOUT YOUR TOUGH
STUFF TO PAVE THE WAY FOR TALKING ABOUT THEIR TOUGH STUFF.

*Nobody is perfect. And the more we talk about the imperfections, the more
we can cover each other's backs and make things happen. These are my
characteristics and where they can show up as gaps—and here's how
you can help me cover them.*

Start with giving. Don't expect reciprocity right away. You are role
modeling, building an emotional bank account, and opening a door. A
long-term door.

Now, to be clear, this isn't an excuse to be a shit. This only works if
your faults don't totally derail the team. If your blind spots impose endless agony on the team and you're talking about them without actively
fixing them, then you're dead before you've even begun.

IF YOU CAN'T MANAGE YOUR OWN DESTRUCTIVE TENDENCIES, YOU HAVE NO
BUSINESS ASKING ONE OF YOUR MANAGERS TO. INSTEAD, STICK TO BEING AN
INDIVIDUAL CONTRIBUTOR.

The outcome: you've built a solid trust-based relationship. You're open
and honest about where you're working and helping. Your team members are too. They know that nobody is perfect. But they also know that
we all have a responsibility to the team to manage self and have each
other's backs.

In the context of this kind of team culture, having a tough conversation is pretty easy. Often, when faced with these situations, I'll set
up time to discuss the issue and give my staff member a heads up that
that's what we need to talk about. Nine times out of ten they bring the
difficult conversation to me because we have a culture of transparency,
accountability and mutual respect. I can expect the conversation to
start something like this: *"Tom, before you start, let me apologize. We both
know I dropped the ball on this."*

Ask yourself how many of your staff members you have a relationship like this with. Because this is what you're looking for. Then you can go into a constructive discussion around root cause and how to avoid the issue recurring. We aren't glossing over it, we are unpacking it and working on it as two adults with a joint goal and vision. We move from tough conversation (parent to child) to problem solving (adult to adult)[15].

Radical candor

A good trust-based relationship opens the door to radical candor. And, as a leader walking a multi-year development journey with a team member, there will be times when you need to be blatantly honest for your message to truly hit home. This is operating with "radical candor". Kim Scott gave the Ted Talk and wrote the book *Radical Candor*. And she is also quoted in a great article in *First Round Review* that is worth reading[16].

The overarching philosophy is that:

TOUGH LOVE IS STILL LOVE.

Sometimes you have to be direct and forthcoming with feedback to hit home. We chatted about my intervention with Natalie in week 2. That was radical candor in its more extreme and risky form—but it worked out. Sandra and I still, publicly, laugh about her moment.

> *I hired Sandra into my first startup to look after and build a coaching and training department. Sandra was young, with good intrinsics, but relatively inexperienced in significant management responsibilities. I spent a lot of time coaching the team on a variety of aspects. I spent a lot of time working with Sandra on numbers and thinking about budgets and projections. I was sitting at my desk when Sandra walked in, stood with her hands together and said: "I feel like my department is under capacity."*

---

[15] From the psychoanalytical theory of Transactional Analysis

[16] https://review.firstround.com/radical-candor-the-surprising-secret-to-being-a-good-boss/

There was a pause as I contemplated all the whiteboarding sessions we had had together to unpack the mechanics of the department, the numbers, etc. This was a confidence thing. Not a smarts thing. Sandra didn't have the confidence to come and tell me "I've run the numbers and I need to hire another trainer." She was holding herself back and needed to snap out of it.

I lifted an eyebrow and played it back in a cold, calm voice: "You FEEL like you're under capacity. After everything we have worked through, you FEEL under capacity?" Sandra, getting the message, turned on her heels and retreated.

Shortly after, one of the other execs walked up to my desk and asked me: "Do you know Sandra is sobbing in the bathroom?"

Yes, I did know. And yes, that was part of the plan. The nice love had made way for tough love. Sandra needed to step out of old habits holding her back and start grappling with some new self-confidence. It worked. And I knew it was going to work because I had the emotional bank account and the radical candor formula for it to work.

THEY SAY COMEDY IS ALL ABOUT TIMING. SO IS EXECUTIVE THINKING.

Fast forward more than 10 years and Sandra and I still giggle about that day. It was a big turning point for her career and her Executive Thinking.

Again, radical candor isn't an excuse to be an arsehole. When used irresponsibly, and without care, you will be being an arsehole.

Facilitative consulting

One thing you didn't see in that interaction is me coaching Sandra by asking her questions. This was a coaching moment—make no mistake. But it wasn't a moment for questions. A lot of coaching best practice is centered around asking questions. And a lot of intermediate managers take this as a prompt to *just ask more questions*. Well, it's a lot more complicated than that. Allow me to present McKinsey's Ask/Tell Matrix.

This super-simple two-by-two matrix is a great mental prompt.

In any situation, you should be making a conscious choice about where you are in the matrix and where you are going. Sometimes you do need to take the path of neutral facilitator and ask more questions to guide reflection. Sometimes you need to be the expert and just explain how stuff works.

In my experience, great executive managers spend 70% of their time being facilitative consultants. Balancing the asking of insightful questions with providing insightful perspectives to build the conversations and the insights together.

	Low ⟶ TELLING ⟶ High
High (ASKING)	Neutral Facilitator | Facilitative Consultant
Low (ASKING)	Observer | Expert

Trying to lead someone to an insight through gratuitous questioning is patronizing.

> THERE IS NOTHING MORE PATRONIZING AND FRUSTRATING THAN BEING ASKED QUESTIONS WHEN IT'S CLEAR THE OTHER PERSON WANTS TO "GUIDE YOU" TO THEIR OPINION. JUST SAY WHAT YOU WANT TO SAY AND LET'S TALK LIKE ADULTS.

Note: The feedback model starts with telling. Not asking[17] .

---

[17] Classic feedback model: 0. Set the scene, gain permission. **1. Provide a concrete observation**. 2. Describe the effect on you. 3. Pause and gain alternate perspective. 4. Suggestion or question for alternative approach/behaviour.

BALCONY AND DANCE AND BACKSTAGE MANAGEMENT

As we have seen, management is a hearts and minds game. As we manage capacity, skill and motivation there are a lot of dynamics at play. And each player in the game has their own universe. Executive managers have to take all those universes into account if they want to orchestrate a high-performance game.

Balcony and Dance, and Backstage Management are two concepts that are powerful mindset shifters. They are quite self-explanatory and work hand-in-hand so let me quickly unpack the theory for those of you who aren't familiar with them:

Balcony and dance

This refers to a perspective.

Imagine you are at a ball. It's a black-tie event with tailored suits and ball gowns. There is a live band playing swing hits from the 1950s. The dance floor is packed. You take your significant other's hand and lead them to the dance floor. You're trying to remember the moves, but it doesn't really matter. Everyone is having a great time. All you really need to do is make sure you don't send your date crashing into someone. What an amazing party!

Up on the balcony, an old lady is gazing over the floor. She is our hostess. She remembers specifically requesting this song when reviewing the set list. Dinner was on time, although the salads did look a little rushed. The bar stock is still going strong (she just checked), and fireworks are scheduled for 12. It looks like everyone is having a great time. What an amazing party...

You get the point. When you are "in the dance" you are focusing on the detailed here and now.

From the balcony you are looking out "over" the people and time to manage the forces at play in the long-term game.

Balcony and dance can refer to group engagements in a meeting or workshop. When to push on a topic or when to let go. You may have been in a meeting where something heated is discussed and the argument is closed without a clear outcome. Frustrating, yes. But maybe there were some balcony forces at play.

You're in a meeting and an executive comes down unnecessarily hard on something that doesn't seem that material. Maybe it's something they are seeing from the balcony that you haven't seen.

Balcony and dance also applies to other areas of management—apprenticing, one-on-ones, tough conversations, coaching—being in a conversation and maintaining awareness of the longer-term process and evolution of things. The long-term game may change what you want to get out of this meeting. The long-term game may change what you say in this meeting. A lot changes when you realize that a meeting is one in a series of engagements and not a one-off.

A simple example:

> *I was discussing semi-annual performance reviews with another exec. We were aligning on focus areas for various key staff members when he stopped and asked: "So, Tom, how do you approach these conversations?" I was initially stumped by the question as a formula/framework didn't spring to mind. Then I realized that that was because the other manager was focusing on the dance and not on the balcony. I responded: "I think about the formal conversation I want to have in six months' time, and I have this conversation to set the next one up for success."*

Dance: I need to have a good performance review discussion in an hour. Balcony: This is another, more formal performance review discussion in the ongoing conversation about Tom's development, growth and performance.

Another example that I see come up all the time:

> I got a call from an executive who wanted some thoughts about a strategy offsite that they were having in a months' time. As always, I asked for the ingoing thinking and plan. She explained how she wanted the theme to be innovation and breaking paradigms.

Now if I had a dollar for every time someone wanted that to be the theme of their strategy offsite... Thankfully, she did not use the term blue-sky thinking *insert vomit emoji*

> It was clear that exec X was in the dance: this is a strategy offsite so it needs to be about the next big thing. It needs to be visionary and "blue sky" and all that nonsense. I brought her up to the balcony and explained: "Your team has been struggling to deliver the basics. They are missing targets and the morale and culture are terrible. So, firstly, your team hasn't earned the right to dream—they need to master the basics or you won't have a team. Secondly, big changes and innovations will make them lose focus on what is important and overwhelm their staff—who could break."

Like always, it was like a veil was lifted. Strategy offsites are a chance to check in. And sometimes checking in means kicking butt, taking your medicine and owning that you've been shit. Then aligning on a plan to not be shit.

OFFSITE ≠ DEFAULT LICENSE TO DREAM

Your balcony view will tell you what the theme of your offsite should be.

If I think back to our discussions about "Pete Factor", much of that can be attributed to Pete being on the balcony while I was fumbling around in the dance.

GREAT EXECUTIVE MANAGERS NEED TO BE IN THE DANCE AND ON THE BALCONY AT THE SAME TIME, ALL THE TIME.

Backstage management

This refers to the smiles that happen in front of an audience—and the temper tantrums that happen in the dressing room.

On stage is in front of the group/team/staff. Backstage is in one-on-ones or smaller groups, linking to radical candor:

> **BACKSTAGE MANAGEMENT IS THE ABILITY TO GIVE AND RECEIVE IMPORTANT BALCONY INFORMATION ABOUT WHAT IS REALLY GOING ON IN THE DANCE.**

If your MOS is your formal management process, backstage management is the informal one. Sometimes pride and personalities are at play. And, by this, I don't mean creating or perpetuating politics. Let me give an example:

Dance: We are discussing the failure of a project to deliver on time. The project manager is, again, running through what is holding the team back and, again, it's more of the same. The broader team is getting very frustrated that the project isn't moving forward the way it should and wants the project manager taken to task.

Balcony: The CTO is derailing the project; the project manager is caught in the crossfire. We are sunsetting a technology that the CTO built to make way for the new tech. It's a sensitive subject and passive-aggressive personalities are making it more complicated than it needs to be. It's a marathon not a sprint—I know we will get there and I understand why the team is losing patience.

Backstage: I set up a couple of one-on-ones with my key managers, explain the situation and ask them to do me a favor and give the project manager a little love for what they are putting up with.

In high-performance environments, a lot can change really quickly. Those changes can be good and bad. And, when you have staffed your team with high performers who care about outcomes this roller coaster can take its toll on them.

Group MOS engagements about this are very important to give clarity, consistency, and transparency to all stakeholders. But personalities are different, and each person reacts to big news differently. Having a good balcony perspective will point you to who needs to have a one-on-one backstage debrief to make sense of the news or change and feel at ease. Not even the best communicators can talk to all personalities, hearts and minds in a speech. And executive managers don't have to; your arsenal includes formal and informal channels of communication—verbal and written.

> **BUILDING YOUR BALCONY PERSPECTIVES, COMPLEMENTED BY VALUES- AND TRUST-BASED BACKSTAGE MANAGEMENT, WILL MAKE YOU A GREAT EXECUTIVE MANAGER.**

MANAGING INDIVIDUALS

I promised not to talk about how to run a one-on-one. And I won't—there are endless e-books on the subject. What I will talk about is the balcony of one-on-ones.

Like your business and function, your staff have different time horizons to be managed on. On one hand, you have the business operating across day-to-day tactics and operations to a broader three- to five-year strategy. On the other hand, you have your staff operating across day-to-day tasks and tactics to broader three- to five-year career and developmental strategies. Putting these together gives a two-by-two matrix, pointing us to four different types of one-on-ones that we should be considering from our one-on-one balcony:

STRATEGY	Quarterly 1:1 strategic business reviews	4 - 6 weekly 1:1 Business strategy update and career development
BUSINESS	Fortnightly 1:1 BAU performance reviews	Apprenticeship: 1:1 working sessions Coaching: Feedback and backstage discussions
TACTICS	TACTICS	STRATEGY

PERSONAL

FORTNIGHTLY BAU PERFORMANCE REVIEW: 80/20 BUSINESS AND PERSONAL TACTICS

This is the standard one-on-one on ongoing operational and project performance. I like to use a KPI dashboard and a simple "highs, lows, issues, priorities and help needed" framework of synthesized points.

Weekly? Fortnightly? Monthly? It depends on the rate of change in operations and results. At the end of the day, if the conversation becomes too frequent to be useful, I change it.

APPRENTICESHIP AND COACHING SESSIONS: 80/20 PERSONAL STRATEGY TO IMPROVE BUSINESS TACTICS

I expect apprenticeship and structured coaching sessions to be monthly (at least). However, depending on what's going on in the business, you may have intense periods of building strategy and/or budgets where the working sessions and feedback opportunities intensify.

Apprenticeship, as we have discussed, is working through strategy and strategic projects together. Coaching would include feedback on observations, retrospectively discussing different approaches to a piece of work or engagement. In my mind, apprenticeship is how to do it. Coaching is how could it have been done differently.

QUARTERLY STRATEGIC BUSINESS REVIEWS: 80/20 BUSINESS STRATEGY TO DIRECT PERSONAL TACTICS

While these can be done in group sessions (like those boring death-by-PowerPoint quarterly business reviews that are institutionalized in some organizations), I like to have quarterly one-on-one check-ins with my managers on OKRs and business strategy.

BUSINESS STRATEGY AND CAREER DEVELOPMENT: 80/20 BUSINESS AND PERSONAL STRATEGY VENN DIAGRAM

These sessions are invariably over breakfast, lunch or a bottle of wine depending on the manager's preference. This is an opportunity to step back and reflect. I put my executive coaching hat on in these sessions. This is a good opportunity to revisit your leadership story and reflect with your manager on how you are doing in the context of your current and next chapters and how the business and business strategy is supporting that. This leads into similar reflections on your staff members professional story, how their chapters are going, how the business is supporting their development and what opportunities may open, and how you are setting them up for success in their next chapter.

I always err on the side of more than less frequent. If I'm not sure, I'll start with a weekly meeting. If that is too frequent to have a good discussion, I move to fortnightly. Then monthly.

IT'S LESS RISK TO HAVE MEETINGS MORE FREQUENTLY AND THEN MOVE THEM OUT. IT'S ALSO MORE INSPIRING TO SAY, "WE NEED TO MEET LESS" AS OPPOSED TO "WE NEED TO MEET MORE."

Talk about leaving

One of the topics that I see most avoided or poorly managed is employees moving on. And part of the reason we inevitably tiptoe through the tulips on this is that we only start thinking about the topic when the employee is halfway out the door. It's like death. It's going to happen to all of us. Not talking about it doesn't mean it won't happen. Not talking about it will just make the surrounding admin a cluster.

> **IT'S NOT A MATTER OF IF AN EMPLOYEE IS GOING TO LEAVE. IT'S ABOUT WHEN THEY ARE GOING TO LEAVE.**

I talk about leaving my job the first time I have a one-on-one with a new manager. I know who I am and what I am good at. I know my leadership story and where this current chapter fits in to it. I also know what the story will start looking like when it's time for me to close the chapter. And that isn't all doom and gloom:

> *I am a startup guy. I like building teams, systems and processes. I work best with management teams under 30 to 40 people. All people managers; not seniors or executives. Above that, things slow down and become more corporate. They need to, to coordinate more moving parts and people. At that stage, my personality becomes too disruptive. At this point, I need to hand over to execs who are better at running businesses in that phase of growth. My work is done. This is a reality. And, when the time comes, it's like institutional knowledge knows it has come, it's the right thing for the business and it's part of evolution.*

If you are clear in your **manage self** and leadership story, it's easy to have the conversation. Then it's easy to ask your brand-new, day-one manager: "So, when are you leaving?" They won't have an answer, but it starts you both working on one.

What do they want to get out of this next chapter together? What do they want to learn and be exposed to? How will the business strategy support that? How will you support and apprentice that? Where can't you help? And, after three to five years together, where are you happily shipping them off to? We will aim for a promotion, another role or an exit to start writing the next constructive chapter.

Easy.

Laying this foundation makes ongoing discussions around satisfaction, happiness, commitment, etc. a lot more structural and expected. Adults having adult conversations.

The optimal length of a chapter

I recently heard of a terrible headline that I think will do a generation a world of hurt: The average millennial stays in a job for 2–2.5 years. Now, let me break down why this is creating amazing glass ceilings for this generation.

Day 0: You start a new job.

Year 1: You learn a new industry, a new team, a new boss, a new product, a new way of working, new technology.

Year 2: You have now been through one annual cycle. The honeymoon is over and now you have your head around how stuff works. The BAU stuff. You're *running* the business well.

Year 3: You can now start really adding value. Drawing from your experience and knowledge of the processes, people and systems— and of the leadership team and strategy through seasons and cycles—you can start weighing in on the more complex stuff that moves the needle. Change, innovation and improvement. You're *changing* the business well: executive thinking work.

Year 4: Building on year three, you're seen as a key team member by leadership. You're a thought leader in your space. Your change and innovations are paying off. You've seen the projects through and realized measurable impact. People come to you for advice. You're apprenticing and mentoring people in your space and in other people's spaces.

Year 5: The *big* promotion.

If you want to keep packing different shelves, fine. If you want to gain deeper understanding on the more complex stuff and accelerate your career, do the hard work. In the high-performance, high-exposure startup environments I have worked in—with all kinds of roles and personalities and skill sets, in intensive learning and exposure environments—this rough timeline holds. It might be 3.5, 4.5 or 5.5 years but it certainly isn't 2.

The three-week rule

An executive I was working with recently was going away for a summer holiday; two weeks' vacation with family. She said, "I am going to try not take my laptop." I lost it.

I understand that in some structures, a team leader needs to be available to manage escalations as a routine part of business. This is typically a lead/manager who has ten or so frontline staff working for them. Even then, I would expect this person to be able to go on leave two to three weeks and have a second in command that can hold the fort. If not, you have a significant management and delegation issue.

Beyond that, managers should be able to take three weeks off, in a cave in Tibet with no Wi-Fi, and have no impact on the business. I have routinely taken three-week holidays to travel Southeast Asia and the like. Not only is this a good acid test of whether I am too involved in the day-to-day business for my role, it is also a good three weeks for my staff to get on with stuff without me.

> FORGET HYPOTHETICAL "GETTING HIT BY A BUS". BOOK A THREE-WEEK HOLIDAY AND LEAVE YOUR LAPTOP AT HOME. IF YOU CAN'T, ASSESS WHY AND FIX IT. ASAP.

MOTIVATING STAFF

Motivation is a mine field. When I first started my management journey, I spent a lot of time trying to figure this one out. These are my learnings and reflections.

BEFORE WE GET INTO MOTIVATING PEOPLE, HOW ABOUT WE REMOVE THINGS THAT PISS PEOPLE OFF?

Niggle initiatives

When I took on my first management role, I ran a comprehensive staff survey to get a sense of how everybody was and what was going on. "The couch" was a hot topic. The company was still small; 30-odd people in total. There was a break area in the middle of the office. There was a couch in the break area. I don't know where it came from but it was shit. It was a clear symbol to the staff: we give our staff "second hand, old, uncomfortable things to sit on when they have a break."

A new couch wasn't going to motivate anyone. A set of round aluminum tables and chairs to be a more appropriate sitting area to eat your snacks and lunch in also wasn't going to motivate anyone. But it would certainly not piss everyone off. So, we got rid of the couch.

I also was *not* going to use replacing an old, f#cked couch as an incentive. I'm not going to patronize my staff by using "average" as an incentive.

These kinds of quick wins are easy to spot. No one holds back on complaining about them. And everyone appreciates it when someone does something about it.

IF YOU CAN'T FIGURE OUT WHAT MOTIVATES PEOPLE, AT LEAST GET RID OF THINGS THAT DEMOTIVATE THEM. GET RID OF THE COUCH.

Another demotivator is under-paying people. Even if they are risk averse and don't leave, they will resent you and be under-productive. Treat people fairly.

Motivation

MOTIVATION IS PERSONAL AND SHOULD BE TREATED AS SUCH AS FAR AS POSSIBLE.

I am a firm believer that money is a ticket to play. Only very specific personality types are motivated by money and most of that is short-term motivation: sales commission and the like. It is always "easy" to put together a bonus scheme or incentives to shortcut good management. It gets old fast.

IN THE LONG TERM, NO AMOUNT OF MONEY IS A SUBSTITUTE FOR GOOD MANAGEMENT AND MEANINGFUL WORK.

So, how do we approach motivation?

Firstly, assess personality types and trust-based leadership. Every person has their own set of priority motivations and core drivers. They often don't know what they are. A curious and insightful executive manager can work with their managers and key staff to distill what this is.

Second is life coaching. Whether this is specific, traditional life coaching or done as part of your MOS, working with staff on their personal goals and aspirations is a win-win.

I'm going to walk you through a dream program concept—not because I think you should start one tomorrow, but because there are interesting insights to gain from it:

I started a dream program in my first startup and it became a backbone of the company culture. We started with the premise that everyone has their own dreams, goals and tangible motivations for coming to work.

I employed a full time "dream coach" (DC) to be the driver and custodian of the program. Participation in the dream program was optional.

You signed up and got a one- to two-hour coaching session per month with the DC. The program was structured as follows:

1. *You write out a list of 100 dreams using the Wheel of Life to be comprehensive. The DC kept you accountable to do it.*

2. *You work with the DC to cut your list down to 25 interesting, inspiring and practical dreams.*

3. *You work with the DC to narrow that down to three to five dreams to prioritize now. We looked for short-term, quick wins as well as meaty dreams that people could start working toward immediately (e.g., buy a house).*

4. *We had a massive dream wall painted with chalkboard paint. Staff were encouraged to write their name and dreams on the wall providing commitment, peer accountability and community.*

5. *Monthly coaching sessions with the DC keep people accountable and helped them plan and make progress toward their dreams.*

The second order benefits to the dream program were that managers could see what their staff's dreams were. They could incorporate the "working on them" in their backstage management, and the "achievement of them" into their onstage management.

We also ran joint events for people who had the same dreams. We taught a bunch of people, including the CEO, how to ride a bicycle. We got a motor-racing set-up in the office for a week. Staff got a session to play if they achieved x target. The person with the highest points at the end of the week either had their driving license costs covered or could sponsor someone else.

When I needed to give a staff member appreciation for going above and beyond, I consulted the dream board to make it personal. We had a backlog in application processing and Busi smashed it out of the park that week to clear it. One of her dreams was to read more, so I bought her the Hunger Games Box Set as a thank you gift.

Great program. Highly recommended.

So, what's next? Know the key motivations of your key staff and managers, and work with them on satisfying those. If you don't have a physical dream board, have one in your mind.

PAY FAIRLY. PAY BONUSES. AND HELP PEOPLE ACHIEVE THEIR PERSONAL DREAMS.

STRESS AND RESILIENCE

We have come so far. I'm sure by now you can appreciate that if you have all the preceding things in place, managing stress and resilience becomes much easier. Even so, stress and associated "freak outs" will happen. Most people have a propensity to expect the worst—no matter how improbable.

> **OUR ROLE AS EXECUTIVE MANAGER ISN'T TO AVOID STRESS—IT'S TO MAKE STRESS MANAGEABLE.**

Let me start with one of my favorite Zen parables to get us in the zone:

There was a wise old farmer who lived in the Japanese hills. He had lived there for many years and had seen many seasons come and go. The farmer had a strong horse; it helped him on the farm to earn his livelihood. As the farmer's son grew up, he helped work the farm and look after the horse.

One night, an almighty storm swept through the mountains, leaving behind chaos and destruction. The barn was badly damaged and the farmer's old horse had run away. His neighbors gathered round sympathetically to help mend the barn, and said, "Such bad luck."

The farmer replied, "Maybe."

The next day, the barn was mended, and the sun was out. The father and son team were toiling away without their horse-friend, when over the hill the horse came galloping, closely followed by a second horse, a strong wild stallion. The neighbors gathered round to marvel at the new horse and enthusiastically said, "Such good luck."

The farmer replied, "Maybe."

Soon, the farmer's son took on the duty of taming the new wild horse so it was better suited to farming. He hopped on the horse two, three times. And on the fourth attempt, he was thrown from the horse and broke his leg. "Such bad luck." said the neighbors.

The farmer replied, "Maybe."

A week later, the army came to the village to draft all able-bodied young men to fight in a terrible war. They went to the farmer's house and saw his son lying in bed with his broken leg in a cast. They deemed the son exempt from the draft due to his medical condition. "Such good luck!", exclaimed the neighbors.

"Maybe," replied the Farmer.

Our farmer was probably named Pete and he had the Pete Factor. The question is: how do we build this in our team members? Like most other management themes: managing stress and resilience is a long-term game.

Rule 0: Manage yourself.

If you're freaking out during stressful situations, your team will know and feed off that energy and stress even more. It is extremely disempowering to see your boss losing it. If you lose it, it's all lost. Play to your strengths: **manage self** and ensure you have the structural support to make it through. If not, you shouldn't be taking on the responsibility to lead people.

Rule 1: Your team must trust you. Be honest with your team—in the good times and the bad.

Nothing impedes resilience more than lack of trust in difficult circumstances. If your team can't trust you, then they doubt you. They doubt what you say. They assume you are hiding things. They assume you don't have their back. Nothing makes a team crumble faster than lack of security. Managing stress and resilience starts with **managing self** so the team knows they can depend on your and follow your lead in the good times and the bad times.

Rule 2: Your team must know that there will be good times and bad times. Life is like that.

While we rally around visions and how we are going to change the world, shit happens. And it happens in surprising ways at surprising times. One of the key messages I have always reinforced with my teams is: *I am looking forward to x. y and z next year. **And I'm very interested to see*** *what surprises come our way.* As Farmer Pete realizes, we will have good surprises and we will have bad surprises. That's life.

> FOR SOME REASON MOST PEOPLE HAVE A FIRM SUBCONSCIOUS BELIEF THAT LIFE SHOULD BE EASY, AND THEY SHOULD NOT FACE ANY CHALLENGES OR DIFFICULTIES IN LIFE.

It may be the lack of a recent world war. Or something else the Boomers did wrong. Whatever it is, it is our job as managers to remind our team that shit happens to everyone and it *will* happen at some point. I am very proactive in sharing my battle scars with my teams.

Rule 3: Your team must know what is at stake.

With all targets and improvement projects and OKRs come the implications of poor performance. You may not know exactly what the implications are, but *this is a business and not a charity*. If we underperform, there are budget challenges, lower bonuses and increases, potential restructurings and redundancies. This is how capitalism works.

Rule 4: Your team must know that you will fight for them – and no one will die if you lose.

Built on **manage self** and **manage strategy**, the team must know that you will go to bat for them. But if you do happen to strike out, shit happens, often, and no one dies because of it.

Do yourself a personal favor and go and find stories of companies that weren't successful. Not because of gross fraud or psychopathic management. Just ordinary companies that got out-competed, or ran out of cash, and folded. They don't get publicized. No one wants that negativity on Facebook. But do yourself a favor and have a look. You will find:

No. One. Died.

People dust themselves off, and find another job, or open another business. All the time. We just don't talk about it enough because it's "negative."

It's actually life. And, it's business.

Rule 5: Be prepared to manage individuals through stressful times.

Leveraging your **manage self** knowledge and personality types, you should have a good sense what triggers your staff and how best to help them feel at ease. That doesn't mean give them false hope or bullshit them. It means helping them see things objectively and with perspective. Like our Zen farmer.

What you say and do can only give people hope if they trust you (**manage self**) and what you are suggesting makes sense to deal with and move past the stress (**manage strategy**)—not make it worse.

Impostor syndrome isn't bad

Impostor syndrome is a sign that you are outside your comfort zone and you're developing. Stress is similar. Stress happens when there is a lot at stake and we are anxious about a negative outcome. Unhealthy stress is when we lose perspective and our emotional response outweighs the logical and probable outcomes and scenarios. Executive managers leverage strategy, scenarios, probability and experience to lead courageously through difficult times and support their teams.

The foundation of helping your staff through stressful times is trust.

If staff are stressed about outcomes *and* they are uncertain about your reactions, support, or whether you are being transparent about broader forces at play, this will make them feel alone and more vulnerable. This is very dangerous. The downward spiral looks something like the following diagram:

As great Executive Managers, we tackle stress differently:

It's okay for staff to be stressed. Stressed and hopeful, not stressed and hopeless.

The first step to managing stress is acknowledging that times are tough, something isn't working the way it is supposed to, or a project is going to be strenuous. Normalizing the experience and emotions can help staff avoid destructive negative thinking like "it's just me that isn't coping." We don't want staff feeling alone and isolated. We have to reinforce and role model that we are in this together.

Second, we should engage on outcomes, especially the negative ones. If this fails, what are the different outcomes that could result? What's the worst that could happen? Even if it means the company will shut down—talk about it. When would we know? How much warning would we have? Will it be a surprise and I find myself out of a job in two weeks? We need to address these head-on so staff aren't left to their own morbid imaginations.

I like to use probability as much as possible in these scenarios. *What are the chances of a) that the company closes, b) you can't find ANY other job in the current market in six months, c) you lose your house, d) you can't stay with family or friends and e) you end up on the streets...?* It sounds extreme but sometimes getting people to play out the irrationality of their fears can help them contextualize where they are now and how far from total doom they are.

Third, we lay out a plan. We consider scenarios and we lay out a good tactical plan. This is when executive managers go into execution mode and are in the trenches alongside their teams. Staff should not be left wondering, *Is what I'm doing right? Is this the best way to help in this situation? Should I be doing more? Something else?* You need to be reinforcing that a) staff are doing the right stuff and b) you are keeping an eye on all the moving parts, so they don't have to.

Staff need to focus time and attention on things they can influence. Being paralyzed by the rising interest rates in the economy won't help you pay your mortgage. Applying for a second job or starting a side hustle will. Make sure the scarce resources of time, focus and attention are channeled toward making change happen.

Lastly, you need to check in regularly to give overall progress and situation updates, on stage and backstage. Don't leave staff wondering if you are going forward or backward. Proactively keep everyone informed of what is happening and whether things are getting better or worse or staying the same.

IF THINGS ARE SHIT, SAY THEY ARE SHIT. THEN WORK TOGETHER TO GET OUT OF THE SHIT.

Hiding stuff destroys trust in the medium and long term. Nine times out of ten, you get through the shit and staff will look back at the process. If you swept stuff under the rug, twisted truths, left out important facts "to protect your staff", it will come back to haunt you.

AVOID, AT ALL COSTS: "IF THEY WERE HIDING THAT FROM ME, WHAT ELSE COULD THEY BE HIDING FROM ME?"

Shit will happen again. And the way you dealt with previous situations will set the scene for how staff will work with you through future situations.

With all your proactive management best practices in place, shit will happen. Surprises pop up. Curve balls fly toward us. We know that, and we have built a management team that has the skills, time and resilience to manage it. Like I said in the introduction, we had 5,000 square meters of office space go up in flames. My resilient and dynamic management team had us up and running within 48 hours. That experience pulled us together more than any other challenge we had ever faced.

Managing staff is an important sphere of executive thinking, but it is only one sphere in the ecosystem. As we discussed, **managing self** and **strategy** are important foundations. The skills and techniques we learn in **managing synergy** and **managing style** will take your **managing staff** game to even greater heights.

MANAGE STAFF TO-DO LIST

- [ ] Build your executive heatmap. Reassess your OKRs for critical gaps.

- [ ] Flesh out your MOS. Define your key sources of information and your macro engagement ecosystem as a weekly, monthly and quarterly view. Assess your one-on-one strategy and schedule sessions to cover any gaps.

- [ ] Design a case interview.

- [ ] Build a 100-day plan for a new key staff member and think through your apprenticeship model for this person.

- [ ] Once a week, reflect on the balcony view of the week and how you can better manage on stage and backstage next week. Put backstage catch ups in the diary.

- [ ] Book a three-week vacation. Leave your laptop behind.

MANAGE SYNERGY

"With silo mentality, organizations lose their collaborative advantage as they are being over managed and under led."

—PEARL ZHU, AUTHOR OF DIGITAL MATURITY

MANAGE SYNERGY IS WHERE ORCHESTRATION AND INFLUENCE TAKE CENTER STAGE. We no longer have the benefits of solid lines, conscious or subconscious hierarchies to manage things.

We start by expanding our OKR horizons to account for the strategies and OKRs of the functions and departments we work closely with. Understanding what's in it for them, and building bridges between that and what's in it for us, is the foundation of good collaboration.

We explore the influencing spectrum, the psychology of influence and influencing tactics. While many of these are used in conjunction or as layers, having a variety of techniques in our pocket and knowing when to apply them (and when not to) makes us a leader among leaders.

We take these learnings and apply them to the practical structuring of workshops. We look at the structural ways to best prepare for and run workshops to drive deliberate outcomes for the hearts and minds of the stakeholders involved.

We expand on this to cover the design of more complex offsites and how we orchestrate energy.

We end by reflecting on how facilitating large group events and problem-solving workshops effectively draws on all of the 5S elements.

THE T OF MANAGEMENT

AS SOON AS YOU BECOME A MANAGER, YOU JOIN A SECOND TEAM—YOUR MANAGEMENT PEER GROUP.

Executive managers are key members of this team. They don't compete with their fellow managers. They don't fear them. They work with them. They collaborate, contribute, and thought lead. They invest as much into building a great management team as they do into building their portfolio team.

Drawing from our manage self learnings, it is equally important to work with your management team to understand each other's characteristics and strengths. You can draw from your fellow managers' strong points, just as they can draw from yours. Having open and honest one-on-one and group conversations around characteristics, team dynamics, and business needs will set you all up to have each other's backs and work together as a unified force.

When you think about your MOS and ideal diary, what proactive engagements and how much time are you investing in getting to know your fellow managers? Over and above a monthly management meeting, you should be having a sit-down lunch with each key manager you work with at least once every two months.

Also think about ways you can structurally use more of the management team to learn and develop. You each have your own stories, experiences, tips and tricks. Why leave it up to chance to tap into these? I would strongly suggest starting an executive masterclass club or similar with your management team. Map out a calendar with a theme for each session. Schedule three hours once every two months. Circulate an interesting *and* useful article ahead of the session and let people know what the theme is. Ask managers to send you any other topics or questions they would like to raise and discuss with the group.

You can chair every one or rotate, don't overthink it.

- Start by explaining the rules/manifesto (e.g., jot down some guidelines around it being a safe space, being constructive, designed to peer-coach personal management issues and not to problem solve joint business issues).
- Start by explaining why you (or the chair) chose the topic.
- Go around the room and get reflections on the challenges people have seen or that they have faced in this area. Jot these down on a whiteboard/Miro. Think human-centered design—spend a little time getting under the skin of the challenges before jumping into solution mode.
- Go around the room again with key takeaways and insights from the article. People can add their own approaches and learnings, tips and tricks.
- Wrap up and synthesize.
- Table other topics for discussion. Let the person who raised the topic present the situation and complication and how they are thinking of resolving it. Let others weigh in and give their thoughts and insights.

Remember, not everyone has challenges in the same areas!

SOME MANAGERS ARE THERE TO RECEIVE AND OTHERS ARE THERE TO GIVE.

Part of this is to share learnings and create a forum for peer coaching. The other part is to bring the team together and build trust and cohesion.

Ten points if it's followed by a wine club meeting... (we will cover this in **Manage Style**).

The OKR Venn

Even if it isn't a widely used framework in your business, bringing your co-managers together to build and understand each other's OKRs is a great way to build a collaborative foundation.

I've used Miro in the past to have one big virtual whiteboard called "OKR mapping"—here we put down all the functional OKRs across the business. Because OKRs are succinct, they are easy and useful to lay out. Kind of like an org chart, but with OKRs. You can draw links and dependencies. You can circle areas that require collaboration and upstream-downstream relationships. This is a lot more specific and tactical than simply a "Let's try working together" approach.

> OKR MAPPING WILL HELP YOU KNOW WHAT'S GOING ON MORE BROADLY AND HOW TO CROSS-FUNCTIONALLY INCLUDE OTHER MANAGERS AND TEAMS IN YOUR MOS AND IN DISCRETE STRATEGIC PROJECT MEETINGS.

Short section. Powerful process and outcomes.

COLLABORATION AND INFLUENCE

I have put these two concepts together as I feel they are two parts to a whole. Let's quickly get theoretical definitions out of the way:

Collaboration: Working with someone, or a group, to produce something

Influence: To affect or change someone in an indirect but usually important way

Why the two together? Well, if you and I were collaborating to build a puzzle, we would need to work together. The concept and goal of building a puzzle are pretty straightforward and commonly accepted by both of us. We may differ slightly on our approach, but the stakes aren't high enough to need to win you over to put the blue pieces on this side of the table.

In business, collaboration is typically more challenging, especially strategic collaboration. Strategic collaboration is working together on strategy, vision, priorities and on delivering cross-functional strategic projects. There is more at stake. The answer is clear and there is no right or wrong. There are trade-offs to be made. Different people and different departments typically have different interests and investments to be made.

So, we end up influencing while we collaborate. And some executive thinking masterminds may even say that "we influence through collaboration..."

The basis of collaboration

Effective collaboration has:

- a shared context
- a case for change (can be shared, or different reasons for different parties)
- a common goal or outcome
- a payoff/incentive for all parties involved

The clearer and more aligned these are, the more effective the collaboration and the harder the team members will work to move up the usual forming, storming, norming and performing curve.

Use your manage strategy skills. Be sure to flesh out a compelling SCR for your strategic project. Use the team to contribute and shape this. Pull in the respective OKRs to anchor the teams. Build the project problem statement worksheet together—pay special attention to the

Criteria for Success section in cross-functional teams. We want to identify, understand and appreciate the benefits for all parties involved.

Hearts, minds and actions

Whenever we are collaborating and influencing, we need to consider hearts, minds and actions. Different personality types are driven by different centers of expression:

- Thinking-centered people need to satisfy their knowledge and logic needs.
- Emotional-centered people need to consider their and others' emotions and the impact on stakeholders emotionally.
- Action-centered people need physical evidence, practical examples, process and steps to be followed/taken.

The influence spectrum

When people approach a new and challenging situation, there is a spectrum of response. You will be met with the same spectrum as you try to influence someone to help you, support you or do something for you.

RESISTENCE	COMPLIANCE	COMMITMENT
• Negative emotions	• Ambivalence	• Positive emotions
• Thoughts "against"	• I may not agree, but fine.	• Positive thoughts
• Actions "against"	• "Do the minimum"	• Helpful actions

Now, we don't *always* need commitment:

> *We are running a strategic project to migrate a core system from x platform to y platform. The project lead is understandably swamped. I have a board meeting coming up and I need an updated project plan. I hop onto MS Project and notice that the plan is out of date. I get in touch with the*

*lead and ask them to update it. I get grunts and groans, but he agrees to update by end of day. I have **compliance** and that is all I need right now.*

*We have monthly management meetings to take stock of KRs, assess priorities and redirect attention and focus as needed. For the past two meetings, I have had to chase up the project lead to get their project plan up to date for the meeting. Not only is it a critical part of the discussion, it's actually the project lead's job to have an up-to-date project plan. It doesn't have to be by the minute, but I expect the plan to be updated weekly to adequately manage the project. **Compliance** is not enough in this case. I need to pull out my influencing tactics to drive more deep-set appreciation for the importance of the plan and get **commitment** on its active use.*

The psychology of influence

Human psychology is complicated but there are a few tendencies that empirically hold true in the realm of influencing. To be fully moved to commitment, a combination of factors is usually at play to fully influence us:

- **Logical proof:** We tend to believe something that appears logical (even if it's not).
- **Authority:** We tend to respect authority and allow it to influence us, even when its source is uncertain.
- **Similarity:** We are apt to go along with people who are like ourselves.
- **Liking:** We more easily allow ourselves to be influenced by people we know and like.
- **Scarcity:** We are inclined to place more value on things that are (perceived as) scarce.
- **Consistency:** We are inclined to keep commitments once we have made them.
- **Reciprocation:** We tend to reciprocate when people do something for us, even if we have not asked for the favor.

- **Social proof:** We tend to follow the crowd and use others' behavior to decide our own.

If you think about a really good sales methodology for a significant investment, consider how many of these strings get pulled in unison.

Different influencing tactics[18]

While there are several different influencing tactics, not all of them are advisable. You'll soon work out why. I'm including them here as I haven't seen them explored enough in business. By running through all of them, I'm helping you diverge and expand your mind. Then, we can converge and figure out which tactics are most useful and when to use them.

Please remember as we explore this list, influencing tactics are seldom used in isolation. Sometimes we draw off a combination in a discussion or workshop. Sometimes we build one on top of the other if we are met with resistance. The categorization is helpful, but they are not mutually exclusive in practice.

Requesting

Simply asking. Usually most widely used by leaders to their direct reports. "Please can you send me your latest strategy pack?"

Stating

Just say what you want or believe. This is quite personality dependent. On one end of the spectrum, some personalities are quite adept at stating an opinion. Others "um and ah" and ask questions instead of saying clearly what they want. Stating looks like: *I believe we should review the remote working policy. The remote working policy isn't working. I want everyone in the office at least three days per week.*

---

[18] A good read is *When Execution Isn't Enough* by McKinsey Senior Partner Claudio Feser.

Depending on the emotional bank account, someone may start with stating what they want and then defer to other tactics once they have a read of the room. I much prefer this than someone taking me on a winding road of logical persuasion without telling me up front where we are going and what their stance is. But I'm a particular personality and I value top-down communication.

Just because you're stating it, doesn't mean I (or others) will agree with it.

However, people may *comply* with it. Assertive personalities often use this tactic with conflict avoiders or passive-aggressives as they know they can get their way by bulldozing others. Not inspirational or sustainable.

Coalition building

This is kind of like leveraging democracy, to a degree. If it's five against one, the one will probably cave in to "peer pressure." Creating a group of supporters of a proposal, using one-on-ones to elicit support leading up to an important decision-making meeting—this is Coalition Building.

Tom has chatted to all his managers and they agree that the remote working policy shouldn't be changed.

Consultation

True consultation is the "ask" quadrant in the "ask tell" matrix. In pure consulting, we are asking others what they think or what they want.

If you had a magic wand, what would you do differently in the next financial year?

You're the head of engineering, what do you think?

We are going to discuss changing the remote work policy in next week's meeting. Please jot down your thoughts and send them to me ahead of the meeting.

Exchanging

You do this for me, and I'll do that for you in return. This can seem manipulative if not used appropriately—think exchanging...

If you give us 30 minutes of your time to for user testing, we will give you a $20 lunch voucher.

Can you help me out on my board pack? I'll give you a hand facilitating your offsite next week?

Rational persuasion

Using logic and good, old-fashioned, cold, hard facts. With strong "thinking-centered" personality types, this can be very effective. For more "emotionally-centered" personalities, it typically won't be enough.

This scientific study shows unequivocally that remote workers are more productive than non-remote workers.

Deductive logic:

Remote workers have limited opportunities to engage in non-work interactions and conversations. Even if they do this virtually, the energetic and subconscious connection is limited. This would impact team connectivity, trust, and overall company culture. If we want a connected, high-performing team, we would need them in the office more often.

Socializing

Socializing tries to capitalize on a person's inclination to be helpful to those they like. You could consider the long-term effects of the emotional bank account and trust as a long-term socializing influencing tactic. However, short-term attempts could look something like this:

Hey. Nice shirt. Is that tailored? Listen, it would be great if you could...

I really liked your presentation on the new operating model proposal. That was well thought out and I can see some real value there. Do you think you could...

Personal appeals

This is often used between parties of social standing.

I could really use your help with...

I need some advice.

Can I ask you to do me a favor?

However, it can infer putting someone on a pedestal if used with someone you don't know.

*I am a friend of Tom's. I noticed you have a wealth of experience in sales and sales management. I could really use your advice and guidance on a strategic problem I'm grappling with..." *insert ego-stroked emoji**

Legitimizing/Appealing to authority

This tactic leverages policies, procedures or corporate hierarchies to apply influence. Sometimes legitimizing is used directly and constructively:

"The HR policy says that we need to follow X process."

"The board has decided we are doing X and not Y."

"Weighing up all the pros and cons, I am making an executive decision to break the stalemate."

Sometimes it can be used indirectly (Threatening as opposed to influencing):

"What do you think the CEO will say if he hears about this?"

Legitimizing is often a scare tactic and should only be used as a last resort. As you can imagine, there is nothing more uninspiring to a staff member or culture than hearing someone say: "I am the CEO and you will do what I say."

ROLE MODELING IS AN INDIRECT INFLUENCING TACTIC

Inspirational appeals

The home of the great executive manager. Think about a viral YouTube video that starts a trend and influences behavior change. Inspirational appeals talk to our core values and motivations, for example:

Tom, I know you are passionate about fitness and growing businesses. Would you coach me to be a better small business leader and strategist?

If something already somehow fits into someone's personal agenda and core values, it won't take much convincing at all.

Executive managers can be masterful influencers by bringing manage self, manage strategy, manage staff and manage synergy factors together.

Different personalities are influenced in different ways

Influence tactic	Type 1	Type 2	Type 3	Type 4	Type 5	Type 6	Type 7	Type 8	Type 9
Consulting	◐	●	●	●	●	●	◐	●	●
Appealing to values	●	●	●	●	●	●	●	●	●
Logical persuading	●	●	●	●	●	●	●	●	●
Legitimising	●	●	●	●	●	●	●	●	●
Exchanging	●	◐	●	●	●	●	●	●	●
Modelling	◐	◐	◐	●	●	●	◐	●	●
Appealing to friendship	●	●	●	◐	●	●	●	◐	●
Socialising	●	◐	◐	◐	●	●	●	◐	●
Stating	●	◐	●	●	●	◐	●	●	●

Legend: ◐ Effective, but selective   ○ Ineffective

Like building trust, if you default to influencing in the way *you most like to be influenced*, you run the risk of being ineffective. Using a variety of influencing techniques, being cognizant of the mindsets and personalities being influenced, and preferably building up to inspirational appeals will yield most success.

DESIGNING EFFECTIVE WORKSHOPS

Strategic problem solving and collaboration are key facets of executive thinking. Hence, being able to run effective and engaging workshops to rally a group around a problem is critical to being an effective executive manager. Here are some thoughts and reflections across the 6Ps of meeting and workshop planning: purpose, payoffs, participants, perspectives, preparation and process.

Purpose: *Why* are we having the workshop? What is the situation and complication underpinning the workshop?

Payoffs: What do we want to get out of the workshop? What do we want others to get out of it?

Again, think hearts, minds and actions. What information do we need to share and grapple with to leave peoples' minds at ease. How do we want people to feel leaving the workshop? What actions do we want to drive as next steps?

Be sure to have a good balcony view on the above. Are we here to inspire change and motivate? Are we here to give the group a reality check—leaving them feeling stressed but hopeful? Are we here to celebrate and innovate? Solve a problem, come up with a plan and inspire joint hard work?

Each of these would inform a different tone, theme and process for your workshop.

Participants: Informed by the above, who should we have in the workshop? Who can contribute? Who needs to make decisions? Who should be part of the process to buy into the outcomes and next steps? Who can add gravitas and authority? Do we need that? Who can add specialist perspectives or knowledge?

Crafting the group is important.

Participant or facilitator: Do you need a facilitator to allow you to be a participant and not run the show? Do you need another manager in the room to play a different role or bring a different energy to the workshop?

Thinking back to influencing tactics: How are you going to appeal to your variety of participants? Who may resist? How are you going to approach the difficult personalities?

Perspectives: How do our participants feel about the subject matter? Are they all equally familiar with the situation and complication? Are we all pretty much on the same page around what good payoffs look like? Or are their different parties with different views?

Are any participants potentially threatened by the discussions we could have or the outcomes of the workshop?

> **SOLID ASSESSMENT OF THE ABOVE ARE KEY TO DESIGNING PREPARATION AND PROCESS.**

Preparation

- Do we want people to prepare offline, unsupervised? What parts of the context can they grapple with to better prepare them for the workshop?

- Do I need to have some one-on-ones to prime people for the workshop? Get support from proponents and discuss how they can support me in the workshop (coalition building)? Work with potential blockers before the workshop so they don't derail the workshop or the energy?

- Do I even want them to be prepared? The more they think about it before the workshop, the more emotionally attached they may be to their thinking and conclusions. Maybe, I want everyone in the room cold so they can all walk the workshop journey together. If this is going to make some personality types uncomfortable, tell them it's by design and not that you have forgotten to send an agenda, or are trying to keep them in the dark. You purposefully don't want them to prepare.

An important component of preparation and process is considering *who* you want to have a voice in the room. Extroverts and bulldozers often take up more of the mic than they should. They open their mouths first and then we either don't hear from the more reserved participants or we run out of time. Thinking about how we tackle this in preparation and in process is key.

You can also use preparation to help you prepare for the ingoing energy and views, and design or tweak the process for workshop. Giving participants an ongoing exercise on, for example, how they feel, what they propose, and what they are worried about can help you gauge the ingoing energy and opinions without having to try to read minds. You can then design your process accordingly. However, this is at the risk of further reinforcing peoples ingoing stances and emotional attachments. I'll run through an example shortly to demonstrate a balance of this.

Process

This is a massively neglected part of the puzzle. We do everything else, then get in a room and start talking. Even worse, we start with an ice breaker. Now it's a workshop! Extroverts love ice breakers. I hate them. In my opinion, there are smarter ways to engage people than seeing their holey socks while they do trust falls. Ice breakers were invented because people run boring workshops.

DESIGN AN ENGAGING PROCESS. FORGET ABOUT THE ICE BREAKERS.

Start with brief context setting and the SC of the SCR[19]. Even if everyone knows why they are there, it helps everyone slip into mental gear. Give a succinct and powerful, top-down, "why we are here." This creates common ground and subconsciously rallies the room around a common goal.

Decide what applicable framework you want to use to center the workshop on. This is "the page" that you are getting everyone around.

- Project planning: use a macro-Gantt chart structure
- Business or product vision: use the BPS framework
- Strategy: use the appropriate strategy framework

---

[19] Situation. Complication. Resolution.

· Define a communication (report, video script, company email): use a pyramid or dot-dash

Using a good framework as a basis will a) help you ensure you are being holistic in pushing the thinking and b) naturally structure the conversation while you keep track of points and managing the room.

THE POWER OF POST-IT NOTES AND THE DANGER OF ONLINE WHITEBOARDS:POST-IT NOTES GIVE EVERYONE AN EQUAL VOICE. USE THEM.

I will put up the framework and say: *Let's start with competitors. Please take some post-it notes and write down a key competitor's name and what you believe they do well. One idea per post-it note.* Give the group two to five minutes. Then start with the introverts! Ask them to present their post-its back to the group and stick it on the board, grouped in the appropriate place.

You get the point. Post-its can help you level the introvert versus extrovert playing field.

The worst thing to happen in a workshop is extroverts jump in, monologue for 20 minutes, and the smart introverts forget the points they had—or don't raise them as they conflict with the extroverts. The post-its strategy overcomes this.

And this is why online whiteboards are limited. Everyone can see everyone else's post-its, preparation notes, etc. And, most often, you only want these revealed in the workshop. So be careful with how you use online whiteboards to get the most out of your participants and process. Here is an example:

I ran a workshop to better define the vision and value propositions for a new tech product. The broader team had given a lot of thinking to it—from multiple angles—and it was time to converge on an aligned and tight view.

Participants would include managerial stakeholders across product, marketing, sales, engineering, customer success, and support, including key

executives. Immediately there is a danger that executive views trump others or that extroverted sales managers overpower others with their "voice of the customer."

We chose the BPS[20] framework (product vision) and a communication pyramid (prioritized benefits underlying the BPS with priority features supporting below).

In preparation, we sent out the BPS framework and asked each member to submit their version 48 hours before the workshop.

*We then **collated** the pieces on a virtual whiteboard. We put all the brand category statements in a group: comparator statements, value propositions, etc.*

*In the workshop, we ran through **each section** individually. Obviously, this was the first time everyone had seen all ten contributions. I didn't want people wasting time reading and processing ten full BPSs. I also didn't want to encourage subconscious voting for which BPS was the best. We wanted all the puzzle pieces on the table so we could build a great, unified picture, together.*

We synthesized commonalities and played them back. We then discussed and debated the conflicts and outliers. We quickly aligned on a great working draft. A "good enough" BPS that we could all sleep on and then polish later.

We then took that and moved onto the pyramid in a similar fashion.

DESIGNING EFFECTIVE OFFSITES

There is a fine line between good workshops and offsites. I get asked about designing offsites all the time; so I'm including it here.

Offsites are obviously different to workshops in that we are taking

---

[20] See Manage Strategy if you can't remember the Brand Positioning Statement.

a bigger chunk of people's time— to take a step back and focus on the bigger picture. We need to hold the energy for longer. The problem solving is generally more abstract and complex. And we are on a bigger stage.

Purpose

Get on the balcony and understand the broader context that your offsite fits into. What is happening in the business more broadly? What is happening in the market? How does this relate to why you are having this offsite and how it should influence the purpose and payoffs. We all want offsites to be fun and exciting and memorable. But, first, they should be useful and effective.

Ask yourself: *I am taking a day/two days out of this teams' month. What are the most important things for us to grapple with to move the needle over the next six months? What should the associated tone be to influence the team while creating urgency and a case for change?*

If you don't need to step back and do big picture stuff, then don't have an offsite. People expect that from an offsite. If you have an offsite and don't do that, it will feel weird. Even worse, you may have an offsite for the sake of having an offsite and distract the team with big picture stuff when they should just be focusing on getting things done. Similar to "Should it be a meeting or an email?" is "Should it be a workshop or an offsite?". Or should it just be a team lunch?

Venue, space and layout

We go offsite to get a fresh perspective, symbolically and energetically. The space we work in impacts how we think and our energy. So, select a space that matches your purpose. I like big windows and spaces that have an open view. Lawns for people to walk on while taking a break or to have breakout sessions around are great. Golf courses and country clubs make great offsite venues because of the space and greenery.

Room layout is important and can change the dynamic. In general, you want people talking to the group and not to the facilitator/you. So, having chairs in a circle with no tables, or a large U-shaped table layout, is preferable to classroom style or one long boardroom desk.

For smaller groups, you can often move chairs away from a boardroom desk to make a circle in a portion of the room.

Seating plan

For certain groups, I allocate seats. If there are two people that are close and like to talk to each other and become disruptive, I separate them.

I make sure introverts don't hide at the back of the room.

Authorities I put up front, near me, so I can stand behind them/put a hand on their shoulder if they take the mic for too long and I want to interrupt them or shorten their monologue.

Sometimes I want certain people together, for example, having a team sit together.

Sometimes I want to spread them out to integrate with others.

Whatever you do, do it deliberately.

Process

Build a detailed run sheet:

A run sheet details the different sections and sessions of your offsite. I like to use a run sheet with the following headings:

- Session name
- Overview of purpose
- Key insights and takeaways to drive

- Format (plenary, small group breakout[21] , individual reflections)
- Bullet points of session flow, including talking points, key soundbites and who is talking/facilitating through the session
- Time allocation (This allows you to manage the macro flow of things and keep track of the details.)

Although run sheets are critical when co-facilitating, it is easy to lose track and forget something when you are in the dance, on the day. A run sheet is a great structural way to revisit the balcony in a session or during breaks.

I build my run sheets in PowerPoint and put them in my main presentation files as hidden slides behind the title slide. That way they are linked to the content and I know where to find them. I have copies on my iPad to refer to in sessions. For newer facilitators, run sheets should be more detailed. With time and mastery, they become more synthesized.

Energy

"So, what was your big insight from the last couple of days?"
I asked.

"That squiggle you did on the whiteboard!", Natalie said.

The squiggle was me talking about the energy we had designed into an offsite run sheet. You need to think about the energy you are designing into your process. Eventually this will become second nature. People can't, and don't want to, sit in a seat for two hours and have someone present slides to them. You can't hold their attention for that long and it's boring. My energy squiggle is me thinking through "when am I talking, and when are my participants talking?"

---

[21] I'm not a fan of random small group breakouts as you get asymmetry in the groups and sub-optimal problem solving. Breakouts in natural teams or departments is fine. These people need to work together anyway.

This happens at a macro level (breakouts, full working sessions) and at a micro level (Tom presents two slides and then we discuss the concepts as a group, for 5–10 minutes, in the session).

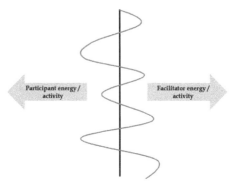

You should also think about macro mental energy. There are three key factors I like to build into my offsite days: foundation setting, diverge, converge.

- **Foundation setting:** either "why are we here and what do we need to achieve?" or "based on these insights from yesterday, why we are here today and what we need to achieve?"

- **Diverge:** explore thinking and frameworks. Offer new thinking and different perspectives to engage the group. People may present their experiences and functional perspectives. What about competitors? Parallel industries? The actual voice of the customer?

- **Converge:** draw insights and key takeaways

- **LUNCH**

- **Diverge:** turning the insights into ideas for action. What are the scenarios? What could we do?

- **Converge:** Prioritize and start defining a plan and immediate next steps

- **DRINKS**

Forum design

This refers to how you are going to design a particular session. Here are some common design options to consider:

- Plenary presentation
- Roundtable presentations from participants
- Breakout discussions around themes or questions
- "Pairing up" exercises
- Gallery walks—rotating small group discussions around stations of information
- Real-time plenary surveys around controversial questions
- Building or playing with prototypes
- Applying specific advanced problem-solving techniques to a problem or proposal
- Co-crafting a communication around the outcomes
- Fireside chat/Q&A

Some are easy and some take time and investment to do well. The point is don't just defer to boring old plenaries and gratuitous breakouts.

APPLY YOUR MIND AND MAKE YOUR OFFSITE INTERESTING AND USEFUL.

Facilitation

And then you need to facilitate. But you are not a facilitator. You are not neutral. You are a thought leader in this space...

FACILITATION SKILLS IN GROUP SESSIONS LIKE WORKSHOPS AND OFFSITES ARE THE CULMINATION OF ALMOST ALL EXECUTIVE THINKING MINDSETS AND TECHNIQUES.

Effective large group facilitation brings a host of 5S elements together to be effective:

- For a start, one must manage self—you must moderate your own personality and characteristics to know when to contribute, when to facilitate, when to simply watch, when to give energy and when to take energy.

- You need to orchestrate the other personalities in the room to ensure that different angles are explored, and different perspectives brought to the table. You need to moderate which voices are heard and to what amplitude.

- As an executive manager, you must manage your own facilitative consulting—when to contribute and guide the discussion with telling, and when to ask questions to build group insight and explore possibilities.

- You must leverage your manage strategy skills and work to ensure the session stays on point. You need to manage diversion and conversion proactively and holistically, to ensure the rigor of problem solving is maintained while not losing time, focus and attention by going down rabbit holes.

- You need to flex your strategic problem-solving skills on the fly—building and exploring issues trees on the fly. Prioritizing where to spend time in the session and where to cover things offline.

- You need to manage staff by providing exposure and education while moving the problem solving forward at an acceptable rate.

- You sit on the balcony while dancing and helping others learn the steps—preparing for the sessions, onstage in the sessions and backstage after the sessions.

- You create and relieve stress to manage the energy in the group while ensuring the tough discussions are had. You have individual, group and faction stressors to juggle.

- You manage synergy by solving for cross-functional needs and ensuring a variety of payoffs are achieved in parallel. You flex a variety of influencing tactics—in preparation, in one-on-ones, in the session and coming out of the sessions to move things forward.

Overall, you make the calls on what to tackle on the field, what to leave for off the field and what to tackle in the next game, to ensure the team maintains their passion for the sport and leaves still hungry for the tournament cup.

AND THIS IS JUST ONE STRATEGIC WORKSHOP. WELCOME TO THE PLATEAU OF MASTERY.

MANAGE SYNERGY TO-DO LIST

☐ Map out your OKRs and the OKRs of the other departments or portfolios that work closely to you on a virtual whiteboard.

☐ Identify which influencing tactics you are naturally most comfortable with and use. Consider your team members and colleagues and which influencing tactics best talk to their personality types. Any gaps or opportunities?

☐ Consider your routine monthly and quarterly meetings. How are you adequately managing preparation, reporting and meeting design to make these *engaging* and *effective*?

☐ Build out a run sheet for your quarterly strategy check-in.

☐ Try out a new (but relevant) forum design technique in one of your upcoming workshops.

MANAGE STYLE

"You can never be overdressed or overeducated."

—OSCAR WILDE

WHEN I THINK OF EXECUTIVE THINKING STYLE, I THINK OF THILO MANNHARDT.

Thilo Mannhardt was the McKinsey hitman. When a McKinsey office was having challenges and the partner group needed a bit of a boost, Thilo was flown in to be office manager. Thilo was the managing partner of the office I joined when I started at the firm.

If you looked up McKinsey & Co in the dictionary before his retirement in 2012, you would find a photograph of Thilo. He always wore immaculate tailored suits, with matching pocket squares and brogues. It was rumored that Thilo had flamingos in the garden of his mansion. No one who met him would doubt that.

As a person, Thilo was incredible. An authoritative leader who knew everyone's name. I wish I knew how he did it. In my first week at the firm I found myself in the elevator. It stopped at a floor and Thilo entered. I averted my eyes, studying Thilo's brogues. He enquired: "So, Tom, how has your first week been?"

Thilo is an Inspirational Leader.

Gary Vaynerchuk is well known in many entrepreneur circles but less so in corporate circles.

Gary came to town for a conference—as one of the headline acts—and my wife insisted we go. I had no idea who "Gary V" was at the time, but judging by the 5,000+ strong audience, he was pretty well known and successful.

The first speaker was an international, award-winning female entrepreneur in a bright and sparkly gold suit that sparkled on stage against the black backdrop. Second was a successful young entrepreneur in a neatly tailored suit. Third was Gary V.

Gary walked on stage in his typical shorts and t-shirt, sporting his signature cap. Now, whether he wears the cap because it's informal and cool, or due to a rapidly receding hairline, who knows? And, frankly, who cares? Over 5,000 people had paid good money to see Gary.

Gary had not prepared a talk. His approach was a "fireside chat" MC'd by someone with a couple of prepared questions Gary hadn't seen before and then mics floated around the audience and he fielded questions.

Gary is an Inspirational Leader.

Now, Thilo and Gary each have their own signature personas. These personas are both authentic but are also carefully crafted to appeal to their audience and to inspire followership.

HOW THEY LOOK, HOW THEY ACT, HOW THEY SOUND, WHAT THEY SAY, AND WHO THEY SAY IT TO ARE IN ALIGNMENT.

Where I constantly see a stark difference between intermediate managers and executives is misalignment in this simple harmony. Manage style complements and is complemented by our other 5Ss[22].

We start with a discussion around inspiration leadership, followership and role modeling. Much of this is greatly influenced by your gravitas and how you hold your own authentic energy.

We unpack what it means to show up, act up and speak up as an executive manager.

We deep-dive into structured communication and the process executive managers should follow to develop and deliver impactful and inspirational communications.

We finish up by talking about "being interesting" and how to work on your own interests and passions to make you a more inspiring person to everyone around you.

INSPIRATIONAL LEADERSHIP AND FOLLOWERSHIP

As you become more senior in an organization, you will experience broader reach—speaking and appealing to a broader company audience. The result you are looking for is inspiring the people who hear you, and eliciting followership.

Followership is just that—people will follow you. They will take what you say and apply it in the right direction. They are happy that they work in a company with people like you. They want to work for you. They want to develop some of your characteristics. You are a role model. A paragon of company vision and values.

This doesn't just magically happen when someone is promoted to executive. God knows, I've worked with some execs that I would only follow into a dark alley to thump them.

---

[22] 5S Model reminder: Manage Self, Strategy, Staff, Synergy, Style.

> PART OF THIS IS FLEXING YOUR AUTHENTIC LEADERSHIP TRAITS AND PART OF THIS IS MOVING OUTSIDE OF YOUR COMFORT ZONE TO BE AWARE OF THE CONSCIOUS AND SUBCONSCIOUS ENERGY YOU BRING TO A SPACE, MEETING, OR EMAIL.

Now, there is a reason I have put manage style last. If you are ineffective at anything we have discussed prior to this, it is going to hurt your style. If you are content free, it doesn't matter how smart you look, the minute you open your mouth, you're done. If people don't trust you, your gravitas will work against you.

Gravitas

Gravitas is bandied about in young consulting circles ad-nauseum, and for very good reason. Step out of consulting and very few people ever hear this important word or the concepts it carries.

> GRAVITAS IS DEFINED AS SERIOUSNESS, WEIGHT, DIGNITY, SOLEMNITY, AND IMPORTANCE. IT CONNOTES RESTRAINT, SELF-CONTROL, MORAL RIGOR, RESPONSIBILITY AND COMMITMENT TO OUTCOMES AND VISION. GRAVITAS IS UNWAVERING. GRAVITAS IS TRUSTWORTHY.

Equally important is what gravitas is not. Gravitas is not sloppy. It's not unsure. It isn't weak. It isn't frivolous, superficial or flippant. It isn't shallow or hesitant or "umm'ing and ah'ing." It isn't childish or child-like.

More often than not, authentic and natural gravitas comes from thought leadership. When I see people naturally and unconsciously stepping into gravitas is when they know what they are talking about, and it is clear in their mind.

The key is to align the planets so that you look like you know what you're talking about, you sound like you know what you're talking about, and your words reflect that you know what you're talking about and inspire action. Gravitas is a function of how you show up, act up and speak up. But before we run through those—a quick circle back to our foundation: **manage self**.

Let's quickly refresh ourselves on the work we did in manage self. What was the leadership style you landed on to describe how you show up as a leader? What are your core characteristics and heatmap? Keep these in your back pocket as we think through show up, act up and speak up. There are also a number of key "no-nos" coming. These hold for all personality types.

When we think of how to push show up, act up and speak up to the next level—looking for opportunities to really build up your leadership style and role modeling potential—this needs to align with your personality characteristics to be authentic and powerful for you.

Show up

Steve Jobs wore sneakers and shorts in one of his most famous videos taken in an Apple boardroom. Steve was worth billions and head of one of the most powerful companies in the world. He had made it. His trust equation had so much credibility and reliability built into it from years of experience, delivery and time in the trenches with his management team, he could have worn a Borat swimsuit. You and I should not. And it's exhausting watching great intermediate managers hit their caps on the executive glass ceiling they are creating for themselves.

Even the smallest things can make an impression. I was once leaving a meeting with a particularly difficult and painful man. We were discussing the energetic void that was his presence when someone remarked: *"He was wearing a wedding ring—so someone, somewhere, at some point, loved him."*

Visual impressions matter. Endless symbology can be attached to the brands you do or do not wear, the jewelry you do or do not wear, your shoes, your wallet, your laptop bag, your car, etc. etc. etc. If you want to be seen to be an executive, you need to stop looking like a naïve graduate.

As with everything we have discussed, it starts with a little self-awareness. And, again, if you want to hide behind your authentic style and be ignorant of the glass ceiling you are creating for yourself—fine. Humans are inherently judgmental, it's a survival instinct. If you don't take that into account, it can work against you.

Quickly back to my consulting days: As I said in an earlier chapter, the client environment for a consultant is most often a hostile one. Everyone, bar the executive who has engaged you, suspects you may be there to fire them. You're an outsider. A potential threat. Many appreciate how much you cost and your broader reputation and are looking for anything they can find to judge you negatively.

This ingrains a lot of self-awareness about how you show up, and the first impression of you. Where you sit at a table. (All) your body language all the time. How you walk. Your expressions around the office. How you talk to the receptionist.

For good consultants, this follows them for life and our "misalignment radars" are well developed. Similarly, the higher you rise in an organization, the more people are going to visually notice and pay attention to you. Make what they see count. Always.

As you turn this radar on yourself (and coach team members on this), here are a handful of examples to demonstrate where I see people leaving style opportunities on the table:

- The laptop backpack: if you work in IT support, great, because that's where it looks like you work. Not in the boardroom. If you cycle to work, get a fancier backpack or a laptop sleeve that you can take to meetings.
- Don't carry excessive shit in your bag/laptop case/wallet. It makes you look disorganized. Why do you even have a wallet?
- Clunky key rings with too many keys on them: get your shit together or keep them out of sight.

- If it has a collar: tuck it in.
- If you're skinny: wear tailored shirts.
- If your shirt doesn't fit: get a bigger one. Buttons shouldn't bulge.
- If you bite your nails: stop. Immediately.
- Excessively high high-heels that you can hear coming from three miles away: you're trying too hard.
- Trousers too short: it looks ridiculous, find a better tailor and listen to them.
- Clumsy? Messy? Sweaty?: Have an extra shirt/jacket in your car/desk.
- Dressing too "fashionably": Great executives generally subscribe to industry-appropriate, timeless-elegance and do not try to make a "hip" statement. They have more important things to worry about. They will make a statement at the polo on Saturday.

There is a reason Tag Heuer models look the way they do in the adverts. Literally, go and Google "Tag Heuer advert."

THE LONGER YOU LOOK LIKE A JUNIOR EMPLOYEE, THE LONGER YOU WILL BE TREATED LIKE ONE.

Excessive over-dressing is equally a no go. But remember, it's easier to take a tie off than to manufacture one out of thin air. The same goes for blazers and jackets. And, if it's too hot, a jacket over the arm still carries the same weight as wearing one.

Ask yourself: What do the great managers and executives above me look like? Then look like them.

BIRDS OF A FEATHER FLOCK TOGETHER.

Take your leadership style and your personality type and spend some time Google-researching leaders and other famous people with those characteristics. How do they authentically show up? Do a Google image search for "professional" or browse professional stock images to find a look you resonate with and you think complements your characteristics.

Two quick different personal examples:

When I work with a client in finance or legal that I know is risk averse, I will purposefully wear a charcoal suit with a tailored shirt and thin dark gray tie. It fits in with what they are used to and doesn't stand out.

When I work with a client in finance or legal that is looking to innovate and try something new, I wear dark designer jeans, with formal shoes, tailored shirt and a designer blazer. This is still formal and very acceptable but it has an edge of "disruptor" and a startup feel about it.

Both styles suit my personality and body type. I'm not wearing a loud red tie or salmon shirt as I don't have a loud salmon personality. If I wore a loud, red tie, it would simply feel wrong to me and my audience. Same as wearing a t-shirt with a blazer. That works for professional playful personalities. Not mine.

How deliberate are you with how you show up? Which audience are you trying to appeal to? And which of your characteristics are you complementing?

Our new virtual boardroom

Your online, home-office or in-office background is a huge opportunity. Virtual backgrounds are inauthentic, distracting, and impersonal. Put a little effort in and make a crafted personal statement.

Start by being aware of what is behind you. Is it distracting? Is it boring? Is it messy?

Google "office background" and get a feel for what is considered a neat, tidy and organized space. Go to Ikea and make yourself one. Less is more.

For external meetings, consider using your company's virtual background with the logo on it. Or, get a high-quality print of your company's logo, appropriately frame it and put it in your background on a shelf/wall. Having a meeting with a senior client who doesn't have a virtual background on? Then turn yours off. Match their energy with the personal, professional energy of your smart, simple background. Don't be lazy. Think it through or find a friend with a design eye to help. It's a small investment that can make huge subconscious and conscious impressions of your character.

The same goes for webcam quality. If you are still using a rubbish laptop webcam that makes you look like a crocodile with your screen tilted up, go and buy an HD webcam. Set it up at eye level, YouTube the "rule of thirds" [23], and look like a professional. It's a career investment.

Act up

Showing up in your designer jeans, ironed shirt, blazer over arm with your royal blue laptop sleeve five minutes late for the meeting isn't going to help you. Paragon is a word that is useful to keep in mind. Paragon is considered to be a person or thing that can be viewed as a model of excellence. In developing toward the C-Suite, it is important to not only know and understand the company's values, but to be a role model of them. These extend beyond the values on a tab on the website. These encompass all the behaviors that make up your company culture. You want to positively contribute to those values and behaviors and help others—especially your team members—exhibit them too.

A polarizing example is lateness.

Being late is a problem for numerous reasons. In the now, it shows disrespect for people who were on time and poor time management on your part. In the broader sense, it impacts trust, shows lack of reliability and control over one's time, a lack of planning and being able to assert oneself to finish a meeting timeously. How can you manage a team to deliver complex projects on time if you can't get from one meeting to

---

[23] **https://www.youtube.com/watch?v=uxIoNL-Uu44** starting at 7:17

another on time? Small things, like accepting late coming, can permeate and materially impact company culture.

I locked our CEO out of a boardroom once.

I joined a company that had a terrible culture of not starting meetings on time. The CEO would arrive 10 minutes late with a cup of coffee in his hand and apologize. Everyone would routinely wait and respond with a "That's okay" when he arrived. This is such a bad cultural precedent. It shows lack of urgency. Lack of respect. Lack of having stuff to do. "I'm the CEO, they will wait for me."

Now, if "That's okay" is your natural, unconscious, conflict-avoidance response to people when they apologize: stop it immediately. Apologies don't make shit behavior acceptable. Especially if it's routine. If a behavior is unacceptable and needs to stop, the guilty party needs to know that, and be held accountable to stop the behavior.

So, one day, I didn't say "That's okay." I locked the door, on the hour, and we had the meeting without the CEO. He was never late again. And you could immediately sense a greater energy and drive in the whole organization over the next few weeks. The coffee break was over. Time to get stuff done.

Back to your leadership style and core characteristics heatmap. What are your personality traits that may impede how you show up and create trust?

- Are you often distracted and late?
- Do you have/know the agenda and are prepared for the discussion?
- Are you overly serious and need to work on generating an authentic smile? (fake smiles are worse than not smiling)
- Do you spend too much time on small talk? Not enough?
- Do you have a "resting bitch face" that makes you seem generally unapproachable?

Have a good think about how your style and characteristics can manifest as physical actions and behaviors.

A great manager of mine used to say, "A fish rots from the head." Staff read and draw from senior leaders' actions and energy. There needs to be alignment and congruency between how we look, how we act and what we say to be trusted, have impact and influence behaviors.

Speak Up

What comes out of your mouth, be it verbal, written or "PowerPointed," is the last critical link in the chain.

ENGAGING WITH IMPACT

Communication is an art that encompasses so much more than just presentation skills. Traditional presentation skills are truly the last you will ever need to master in business, unless your business is motivational speaking.

Communication draws off everything we have learned until now. Communication starts with **manage strategy**. You cannot be an effective communicator if you don't have anything useful to communicate or you are not asking insightful questions. This is a key foundational point. I see so many managers getting caught up in *how* they are going to communicate something when they should be focused on *why* and *what* they are communicating.

Manage self: am I the best person to communicate this? Does my audience trust me? How do I need to adapt my style to cater for my characteristics and communicate this with impact?

Manage staff: what's happening from the balcony? What dance is the audience doing?

Manage synergy: how am I going to influence? What energy do I need to carry? What energy does the audience already have?

> GREAT COMMUNICATION DOESN'T MAGICALLY HAPPEN. IT'S GREAT
> BECAUSE IT'S DELIBERATE.

The development of any communication—even a text message—should pass through these gates:

- Purpose
- Structure
- Content
- Clarity
- Flair

Purpose

This obviously answers the overarching why. However, we need to think of second-order purpose factors related to our audience:

How does my audience feel about the topic? How do I want my audience to feel? (hearts and minds)

Do I need to influence my audience? What are the key personality types and what influencing tactics may be appropriate?

WIIFM? and what's in it for them (WIIFT)?

Structure

There are two key elements of structure: how you build a communication and how you deliver communication:

The Pyramid Principle [24]

Building a communication pyramid is very helpful to organize and prioritize your thoughts for communicating. It is also a great tool to collaborate on messaging and communication. The idea behind the pyramid was made famous by Barbara Minto in the 1980s and I continue to use it to great effect.

---

[24] Barbara Minto published the book back in 1987: The Pyramid Principle: Logic in Writing and Thinking. Ironically, I don't think it's an easy read. Go figure.

The concept behind the pyramid is that your **key** pieces of information lie at the bottom. Your key pieces of information, not all your information! Using our why, we prioritize what we know and decide what is most useful to include in our communication. We then organize and group these pieces of information into governing thoughts: these are the key so-whats or insights we can gain from the information below.

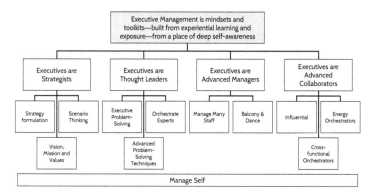

These governing thoughts then roll up to the top of the pyramid to give us our overarching so what—our key message.

I've included an example on the previous page: Assume I am writing an article or giving a 60-minute talk on the topic of this book. I could choose one of the Ss to talk about. I could choose all. In this instance, I have left out the last S (due to space to be honest) but you can see how I would organize my thoughts and package the bottom topics into governing thought "buckets."

This is, fundamentally, how I built out the 5S executive thinking model.

I originally started with the classic: lead self, lead others, lead business. But it was lacking the specific nuances of strategy and failed to differentiate between managing team (direct line) and non-direct line "others." So, I rebuilt the pyramid to be more insightful.

What is critical to note, is that there is no *perfect pyramid*. There are good pyramids and there are bad pyramids, sure, but the pyramids effectiveness lies in its use. Gather your thoughts, nail down the key insights you want to deliver, and then move forward to develop the story.

Synthesis vs summary

This topic should have been an entire chapter—maybe even a book. Nothing frustrates a great executive more than people's inability to synthesize information.

Summary: an abridged version of the original. The same information but in shorter form.

Synthesis: Insight. What is the information telling me? What is the "so what?"

Example:

Summary: The initial discovery and design activities took a week longer than we had anticipated. This seems to have been incorrectly scoped in the initial sales process. We are working on increasing capacity in the project team—specifically the engineers—to speed up the implementation phase.

Synthesis: Shit happens but we will still deliver the project on time. The surprises couldn't have been seen by the sales team.

Appreciate this: If someone gives you a summary, *you must do the work to synthesize it.* And, with incomplete information you may draw the wrong conclusions or insights.

> SYNTHESIS ADDS VALUE. SYNTHESIS IS THE EXECUTIVE ANSWER OF "SO WHAT?" AND "WHAT'S NEXT?" EMPLOYEES ARE PAID FOR SUMMARIES. EXECUTIVE MANAGERS ARE PAID FOR SYNTHESIS.

Link to the pyramid? **Each move up the pyramid is a synthesis of what is below.** Be a synthesizer, not a summarizer.

Now that we have our pyramid, how do we communicate it?

Top-down communication: We start at the top!

I can't blame people for starting at the bottom. Throughout school we are encouraged to communicate using the "scientific method" or to "show your workings." This isn't school anymore.

WE KNOW YOU'VE DONE THE WORK. START WITH THE PUNCHLINE.

I'm an executive manager. I understand why we are here, and I have a fairly good view of the business. Start with the top of your pyramid—your overall insight or big idea. If I agree with you—done! Sold! Moving on.

If not, we can move down whichever supporting blocks of the pyramid I want to interrogate further or explore a missing set of blocks.

There is truly nothing worse than getting into a meeting and someone starts a once upon a time monologue—starting at the bottom of the pyramid and wanting to cover everything they have thought about and learned—before getting to the big crescendo of their point. It's inefficient. It's boring. It diminishes your impact. Don't do it. Please.

The elevator pitch

You may have heard of this idea but few people appreciate the second-order insights.

First, the premise behind the concept is: You arrive at work. You get into the elevator. Just as the doors are about to close, the CEO walks in and says, *How is it going with x project?* You now have 22 floors or 30 seconds to give the CEO your synthesis.

The idea is to force top-down insight delivery. What does the CEO care about? What is the headline? What will have impact?

Second order insight: where I see people get this wrong is that they *try to summarize.* And they get caught up in "what are the fewest number of words I can use to get all this information across." When someone gives me a good elevator pitch, it's because *they know what the key insight is.* If you are crystal clear in your mind on what the key insight is, you can give an elevator pitch in your sleep.

> *The project has had its speed bumps but will be delivered on time. There is nothing we need to systemically fix from the learnings.*

AN ELEVATOR PITCH IS A PROBLEM-SOLVING TOOL. IT'S A LIFESTYLE. IT'S BEING AN EXECUTIVE MANAGER.

If you always have a good elevator pitch in your mind, it means you know what the key insights are! It means you are on the problem-solving balcony. Stepping back and coming up for air daily, weekly, monthly to distill the elevator pitches of what's going on in your portfolio is key to being in control and key to driving the right "what's nexts."

> *Let's quickly go back and revisit my introduction to Natalie. Remember, we sat down, she opened her spreadsheet, and started walking me through it— cell by cell.*

> *This breaks all the rules above and this is why I interrupted Natalie and gave her a top-down, synthesis intervention. She is an executive. I wanted her to communicate like an executive. Job done.*

The story

Sometimes we want to communicate more than just the elevator pitch. We still want to know what the elevator pitch is but we want to add more flavor to our communication to a) better communicate to hearts and minds and b) influence different personality types and people with different contexts.

The tools I use here is the SCR and the dot-dash.

We went through the SCR framework in **manage strategy** and developing our strategic narrative. Laying out situation—complication— resolution *is not top-down communication*. We use it when we want to weave a story together. When we want to take our audience on a journey and/or we want them to be aligned on the important elements of the journey in the context of the resolutions we are about to give them.

There are other ways to build a story— stacked SCRs, CSR, RSC — depending on your purpose and intention.

The dot-dash

The dot-dash helps us plan out our story and get a richer view of our SCR (or whatever) before we get lost in words.

The idea is simple. Open a document and write the contents page. The **dots** are the main ideas or big sections, and the **dashes** are the supporting ideas. For a speech, an article or report, the **dots** would be the main ideas per section and the **dashes** would be each paragraph. For a presentation, the **dots** would be the slide and the **dashes** would be the ideas you want to convey on each slide.

Here is a simple example for this section of the book. I've been doing this for years, so I organize words and phrases. When you are new to this, or when you really need to pay attention to the emotive side of the communication, it's worthwhile using full sentences.

Engaging with impact section: dot-dash
- *Link to 5S and why it's so late*
- *5 step comms development process*
- *Purpose*
  - *Why*
  - *Influence*
  - *Audience*

- *Structure*
  - *The pyramid principle*
    - *synthesis vs summary*
  - *Top-down comms*
    - *the elevator pitch*
  - *The story*
    - *dot-dash*
- *Content*
- *Clarity and Specificity*
  - *Gunning Fog Index*
- *Flair*
  - *Analogies*

Content

The bottom of the pyramid is as important as the top. Your information, analysis, prioritization reasoning, context, and complications are all important foundations for your arguments. You need to make sure your insights and recommendations are well supported by rigorous problem solving and executive manager thinking.

We know you're smart. We know you've worked hard. You don't need to communicate all of it.

Clarity and specificity

All the above is a waste of time if you can't communicate clearly. And I don't mean simply avoiding "umm" and "ah."

Purpose and logic first: Don't start with the storytelling. Don't start with some PowerPoint infographic that has nothing to do with the purpose and intention of what you are trying to say. It's distracting. It's amateur.

Start with logic and bring everything back to purpose and logic: structure, content and looks.

Simple language: You are not JK Rowling. And, in all likelihood, JK Rowling would be terrible communicating in the boardroom. Use short, active sentences. Look it up. Use verbs. Look those up. Learn about the Gunning Fog Index and use it. Less is more. Always.

Short sentences: For every sentence, ask yourself if you can make it two sentences. Don't try to make one sentence into two sentences. Just make sure two sentences are two sentences. A sentence that turns into a paragraph with commas and ands and dashes is shit. If I must read a sentence three times to understand what you are trying to say, I won't think you're smarter than me. I'll think you're a shit communicator and I'll stop reading. Life is short. TL:DR.

Insights, not waffle: Focus on the top of the pyramid. And focus. Focus. Then talk. Then stop. Don't feel the need to fill in pauses. Ask a question of your audience if you must. Don't keep talking unnecessarily. Make your point and stop. Please.

Engage, don't read: PowerPoint slides are there to support the conversation. A slide is a visual reinforcement of the short, punchy, insightful narrative you're giving us. They are not your speech notes. They are there to help us "get it quickly" and remember through visual learning.

STRUCTURE. STRUCTURE. STRUCTURE.

Punchlines and sound bites: What is your "Start with why"? Craft simple and insightful sentences to really land your points. Prepare the one-liners your audience can take and use impactfully.

Be specific: Speaking in generalizations (or hyperbole) doesn't drive insights.

The new remote work policy is a nightmare.

The IT project took too long and used up too many of our resources

Which IT project? How long? Which resources? Compared to what benchmark?

The SAP implementation overran by 40% and used 200% more project FTEs, compared to a typical project of that scope.

Thank you :)

If the first question out of your audience's mouth is *What does that mean?* or *So, what do you want to do?* you've failed your audience and in your credibility as an executive manager.

Overall, DON'T:

The implementation phase of the transformation initiative is vitally important to overall program success in line with our customer service agreement, so we should leverage our core competencies to drive end-user engagement, excitement and adoption of the technologies.

DO:

Let's pull out all the stops to make sure the team is using it and excited about it.

Flair

Flair comes last. Once you have nailed down all other components of good communications, you can consider flair.

Flair is flavor: examples, stories, analogies, infographics, icons, symbolism.

HOW CAN WE ADD RICHNESS TO OUR COMMUNICATION THAT SUPPORTS OUR PURPOSE?

The first question is *Do we need the flair-factor at all?*

I've seen far too many proposals and presentations where the flair-factor has undermined the intent. Using the wrong symbolism, an obscure story, or an infographic that doesn't correlate can make you look like you're trying too hard. It can grossly undermine your credibility. Especially to seasoned executive communicators.

The problem with the flair-factor is that it is binary: you can either get it very right or you can get it very wrong. If it's important enough to add flair, engage with flair-masters[25] so you get it right.

Any and all communication—an announcement to the team, the whole company, an email, a Board report, a presentation—should be approached with:

PURPOSE > STRUCTURE > CONTENT > CLARITY > FLAIR

Your authentic communication style

By now, you have a very good understanding of my communication style. And my communication style is a direct reflection of my personality type. I'm direct. I'm not a comedian. I have a dark and dry sense of humor. I can be succinct to a fault. I don't tip-toe through tulips. My engagement, communication and presentation styles need to take all of that into account.

If I tried to stand up and deliver a presentation or speech like Richard Branson, I would fail. I simply cannot smile for that long. I don't laugh that much. And if I tried, my audience would see right through me and that would destroy my credibility and trust.

SIMILAR TO MANAGING SELF, I NEED TO CATER FOR MY INHERENT CHARACTERISTICS TO BE AN ENGAGING COMMUNICATOR.

---

[25] https://www.toastmasters.org

The first step is to understand what kind of communicator I am. This links very closely to leadership style. We can take our management heatmap and think through how we leverage those characteristics to make our communication more impactful. And we can look at our hotspots and apply our minds to what we should avoid or introduce to ensure they don't hinder our intent.

We can take our personality type and look at great leaders and famous personalities to see how they authentically communicate. For actors and actresses, we can look at how people are typecast.

Get structured feedback using the above. We can seek out coaching opportunities. Observe yourself! Record meetings, presentations and speeches to your team and company.

If you're stoic, be a great stoic communicator. If you're an enthusiast, be a Richard Branson-level enthusiast.

But, again, only after you're sure what's going to come out of your mouth is on point.

BEING INTERESTING

This is more of a higher-grade executive thinking characteristic. I am including it here as it's part of the long-term game and the sooner you figure this out, the happier I believe you will be.

CONTRARY TO LINKEDIN'S VISION AND MISSION, YOU ARE MORE THAN YOUR PROFESSIONAL ACHIEVEMENTS.

Having hobbies and interests outside of work enriches your life on many levels. You can learn and develop in an environment that doesn't directly link to your salary and survival. You can learn new skills and be a beginner over and over again. You meet new people from all walks of life and broaden your perspectives and network. And, maybe most importantly, you have more interesting stories to tell on Monday!

Scenario 1

How was your weekend?

Fine, thanks.

Scenario 2

How was your weekend?

I skydived out of a hot air balloon.

I ran my first 21 km race.

I crocheted a blanket for my new grandson.

Anything but *fine, thanks!*

Try stuff. If you don't know what you're interested in, grab a friend and make a commitment to try five new things in the next year. They don't need to stick. You don't need to master anything. Just try stuff, meet people, make stories. When I left consulting, I committed to properly learning a new hobby every year. And I have met some amazing people and have some amazing stories and perspectives as a result. It all started with a list of 100 dreams.

100 dreams

As mentioned in manage staff, I was introduced to The Dream Manager by Matthew Kelly back in 2010. Part of our dream program was to write out a list of 100 dreams.

One. hundred.

It's an amazing exercise. 10, easy. 20, okay. 30+? Now you're digging into all the nooks and crannies of your 12-year-old self and all the things you have ever dreamed of doing.

When I was a kid, I wanted to learn to sketch. Properly sketch. I had forgotten all about that. It landed on my list. I was chatting to a potential business partner, and she mentioned that she was going to art classes that evening. Fast forward a couple of weeks and we were drinking wine at art class together. Now I travel with an iPad pro and sketch while I fly. I find it very meditative and rewarding. I've started hundreds of sketches I've never finished; but I love the process.

When I initially wrote my list of 100 dreams, I used a good old-fashioned notebook and pen. It took me a couple of weeks and I carried my notebook around to coffee shops and meetings and so on. I found and reviewed the list around 10 years later and I was amazed at how many dreams I had accomplished.

I would strongly encourage you to write your list.

- Start with a brain dump of current ideas.
- Then walk through your life. What did you want to be when you grew up? What were your dreams at high school? University?
- Then refer to something like the Wheel of Life and think through the different aspects of life to make sure your list is holistic.

Then prioritize and get going!

Bring your interests to work

My desktop background is a photo of me jumping out of a chopper. My wife took the photo while jumping out of the other side. Many a conversation has started because of that photo. Thanks @GoPro.

People never really know what I will answer to *How was your weekend?* but they know it will often be interesting.

Part of being an inspirational leader is being an inspirational person. Being aware of your passions, acting on them, and doing cool stuff inspires other to do the same. And it makes for fun conversations.

Defining your organizational contribution

Contributing more broadly than just your job or role description is part of the executive role. Great executives look for ways to further the company mission and culture beyond their core role and portfolio. They also enjoy doing it: bringing their personal passions to work makes work more fun for themselves and for other like-minded people.

I know people who have started a band with colleagues.

Others started a chess club.

I started a wine club.

I took colleagues skydiving.

We taught our CEO and other staff how to ride a bicycle.

Thinking through your leadership style, your natural strengths and talents, your interests, hobbies and passions—where can you have more fun and contribute to your company and colleagues?

Finishing in style

That wraps up our 5S Executive Thinking Model. Manage style encompasses all other elements and defines your leadership essence as an executive manager, whether it's in one-on-ones, problem-solving sessions, facilitating workshops, walking around the office or the Polo Club on Saturday.

This is not your internal dialogue. It's not who you want to be. It's how you currently show up, act up and speak up every day and how your interests and passions make you a more interesting colleague, a leader and an inspiration to others.

As you have discovered, the 5S framework is an ecosystem. As you move up the slope of enlightenment in one sphere, it will flow over to make you more effective in the other spheres. This is because executive thinking is about thinking. It's about perspectives and mindsets. The more you can open your mind's eye to the broader components and possibilities across the 5S's, the faster you will elevate your executive thinking game.

MANAGE STYLE TO-DO LIST

- [ ] Assess your "show up" factors, including your home-office background. Determine what you can change to immediately increase your gravitas.
- [ ] Build out a pyramid and dot-dash for an important presentation or working document.
- [ ] Write down your elevator pitch for an important piece of work or OKR.
- [ ] Define your authentic communication style and persona.
- [ ] Write a list of 100 dreams. Prioritize five. Take up a new hobby. Jump out of an airplane.
- [ ] Start an executive book club.

CONCLUSION:
THE 5S ECOSYSTEM

I NITIALLY, WE CONSIDERED THE 5S JOURNEY TO BE A PYRAMID. As we start tackling this framework, a solid foundation of self-leadership and then thought leadership is paramount. Without knowing how you, personally, influence the world around you, you are hamstringing every other sphere of executive thinking. As we discussed, being an awesome person who is not aligned with business strategy or able to support your people with thought leadership makes you a great golf buddy—not an executive manager. As we begin to develop and master the five spheres, it's clear as day that they form an Executive Thinking Ecosystem.

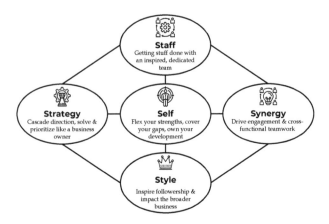

How I show up and act up influences how I build trust and emotional bank accounts.

Balcony and dance perspectives help me flex or hold back my personal characteristics in any and all engagements. It becomes natural: subconscious.

Strategy and scenario planning helps me design and facilitate effective cross-functional problem solving, workshops and offsites.

Being aware of and mastering offsite energy helps me plan great holidays (without my laptop), incorporating the awesome new hobbies I picked up exploring my list of 100 dreams!

AS ANY GOOD EXECUTIVE MANAGER WOULD ASK: WHAT'S NEXT?

As an overarching philosophy, we move from manage to lead—being a powerful senior facilitative consultant that leads others on their executive manager journey. From managing the 5Ss we move on to leading others (from junior to most senior) in how they manage their 5Ss.

SEE ONE. DO ONE. TEACH ONE.

From managing self to leading others to better manage self. Mastery of different personality profiles, and how these can be structurally supported in the workplace to optimize performance.

From managing strategy at a department and functional level to leading the development of business and corporate strategy. From managing effective problem solving to leading strategic problem-solving using advanced problem-solving techniques.

From managing staff to leading the orchestration of functions and business units; evolving broader business structures and operating model; leading MOS philosophy changes and leadership succession planning in line with proactive culture orchestration.

From managing synergies to leading the creation of new synergies—developing new functions, departments and products, business partnerships, mergers and acquisitions.

From managing style to being a unique paragon of values and inspiration that fits the company culture and era.

As I said at the start of our journey, the older I get, the more complicated I realize the world is. There is no end to our own personal journeys from manager to executive manager to executive leader. You will always face new, exciting and daunting opportunities and situations. You will always face new and more interesting and difficult people.

The key acid test for executive thinking at every level, in every sphere, is:

IS IT INTERESTING AND USEFUL?

Is it going to push the problem solving and move people forward today? Are we overcoming the next bottleneck in thinking? And are we inspiring those we work with to achieve meaningful success?

ALL IN ALL, I TRUST YOU CAN APPRECIATE THAT EXECUTIVE THINKING ISN'T SOMETHING YOU DO. IT ISN'T A TOOLKIT. EXECUTIVE THINKING IS A LIFESTYLE.

I'll see you in in the boardroom.

EXECUTIVE THINKING CHECK LIST

MANAGE SELF

☐ build authentic trust quickly and effectively

☐ know your core characteristics and own how and when those can be destructive

☐ set yourself up in the right roles and ecosystems to play to your strengths, focusing on the long-term success of yourself and the business—don't try to "fake it 'til you make it"

☐ have a compelling leadership story

☐ know what's next for you and your people

MANAGE STRATEGY

☐ join the dots between company strategy, functional strategies and department strategies

☐ have a compelling narrative about how your team got here and what your team needs to focus on

☐ think "what's next"

☐ don't wait for things to happen—get stuff done. The right stuff

☐ be a thought and problem-solving leader—if you don't know the answer, lead structured efforts to find the answer

MANAGE STAFF

- ☐ be the custodians of their portfolio's vision, mission and values
- ☐ build effective high-performance teams with the right mix of smarts, culture and personality types
- ☐ facilitate compelling career journeys for your high performers
- ☐ manage from the balcony and in the dance; on the stage and behind the stage
- ☐ manage energy, focus and resilience as finite resources in a long-term game

MANAGE SYNERGY

- ☐ manage your exec team
- ☐ join the dots across portfolios to drive business synergy
- ☐ be a great influencer, see org chart lines for what they are
- ☐ master the art of collaboration—target hearts and minds
- ☐ make working together meaningful and memorable

MANAGE STYLE

- ☐ understand your broader conscious and subconscious impact
- ☐ have gravitas and inspire followership
- ☐ be interesting
- ☐ be clear and succinct
- ☐ be dynamic and engaging

NEXT STEPS

- Complete your Executive Thinking Scorecard at **www.themanagementdistillery.com.**

- Apply to participate in one of Tom's exclusive Executive Accelerator Programs.

- Review this book on Amazon.

- Have great impact. Inspire your people. Be yourself.

ABOUT THE AUTHOR

TOM GARDNER is a startup COO. He has scaled three startups and co-founded two. He has multiple entrepreneurial ventures and consults to some of the world's biggest corporations.

Tom got a wealth of early experience in the "executive toolkit" at McKinsey & Company. Here, he worked with global leaders across industries, functions and continents on strategy and organizational topics. Tom got heavily involved in learning and development at the firm, training and coaching consultants to be "McKinsey Consultants".

Tom then found his niche in running and scaling start-up operations—pulling together corporate strategy, functional strategies and high-performing management teams to rapidly solve problems and have impact.

The golden thread? Tom is driven by building great managers and executives. No matter what venture, consulting engagement or bottle of wine Tom is involved in, leadership development and coaching are always a core part of the conversation.

NOTES

NOTES

Printed in Australia
Ingram Content Group Australia Pty Ltd
AUHW011105060624
395393AU00002B/2